THE QUEEN'S NANNY

BY MELANIE TAIT

CURRENCY PRESS
The performing arts publisher

ENS
THEATRE E
MBE
ML E

CURRENT THEATRE SERIES

First published in 2024
by Currency Press Pty Ltd,
Gadigal Land, Suite 310, 46–56 Kippax Street, Surry Hills, NSW 2010, Australia
enquiries@currency.com.au
www.currency.com.au

in association with Ensemble Theatre

Typeset by Brighton Gray for Currency Press.
Front cover shows Elizabeth Blackmore.
Cover photography by Brett Boardman.
Cover design by Alphabet Studio.

Currency Press acknowledges the Traditional Owners of the Country on which we
live and work. We pay our respects to all Aboriginal and Torres Strait Islander Elders,
past and present.

A catalogue record for this
book is available from the
National Library of Australia

Contents

THE QUEEN'S NANNY   1

Theatre Program at the end of the playtext

The Queen's Nanny was first produced by Ensemble Theatre, Cammeraigal Country, Kirribilli, on 6 September 2024, with the following cast:

J / NANNY / BERTIE / AINSLIE / LILIBET / GEORGE / BRUCE GOULD	Matthew Backer
MARION	Elizabeth Blackmore
ELIZABETH	Emma Palmer

Director, Priscilla Jackman
Assistant Director, Miranda Middleton
Set Designer, Michael Hankin
Costume Designer, Genevieve Graham
Lighting Designer, Morgan Moroney
Composer & Sound Designer, James Peter Brown
Dialect & Voice Coach, Jennifer White
Movement Coach, Tim Dashwood
Stage Manager, Sean Proude
Assistant Stage Manager, Madelaine Osborn
Costume Supervisor, Lily Mateljan

CHARACTERS

ELIZABETH

MARION

J

BERTIE

NANNY

AINSLIE

LILIBET

GEORGE

BRUCE

NOTE ON THE TEXT

The Queen's Nanny is written for three actors. Ideally, one actor plays ELIZABETH, one plays MARION and a third actor plays J and all other parts.

When characters address the audience, it is marked in the directions as narration. When characters address each other, it is marked in the directions as dialogue.

— means the line after can interrupt.

'papa' is pronounced 'pa-*pah*'.

There isn't an intermission, please don't insert one.

This play text went to press before the end of rehearsals and may differ from the play as performed.

1. A TEA PARTY, AGAIN. 1980S/PURGATORY

MARION *is preparing to welcome someone to tea. She's done it many times before.*

There's also a carpet bag of treasures she lays out. They're mementoes important to her prospective visitor: letters bound by ribbon, photos, a battered copy of Black Beauty.

J *watches her for a while before saying anything.*

J *narrates.*

J: There she is.
    Laying the table. Putting out her finest doilies.
    The loose leaf ordered from London.
    Just in case.
    For a tea party that will never happen.
    You think you know this story.
    You've probably looked it up before coming tonight.
    But the thing is with stories: they change.
    They change in the telling. In the distance from the telling. In the person doing the telling.
    Apparently, the questions are the same every summer.
    Over so many summers.
    'Will She stop her car?'
    'Will She open the gate?'
    'Will She come in?'
    'Be embraced?'
    'How long it's been!'
    'How good you look.'
    'Come in for tea, for cake, let's remember a time that's passed us by.'
    Once the tea is prepared, she watches from her window.
    Marion Kirk Crawford watches.
    And watches.
    And watches from her window.
MARION: Of course I watch from my window.

This window is in prime position.
Anyone who drives between Aberdeen and Balmoral?
They have to pass by my window.
So why wouldn't I watch from my window?
It's my window at the front of my house.
I bought it with my money.
I'll watch whomever I want, whenever I want, from whatever damn window I please—

J: Here they come.
What she's waiting for.
The cars: newly polished, especially for this trip.

MARION: Police escort out the front.

J: Police escort out the back.
Of course, we all know who's driving the old Land Rover in the middle.
It's Her.

MARION: Of course it's Her.

J: It's really Her!

MARION: Why else would there be such a fuss?

J: I've never been this close to Her!

MARION: It's exciting, isn't it?

J: I can see Her in that car—

MARION: Are they slowing down?

J: They're not slowing down.

Dialogue.

MARION: They're slowing down.

J: They're not.

Narration.

She drives right past.
Past the doilies.
Past the loose leaf ordered from London.
Past her.

MARION *is upset by the passing cars. She takes one of the cups and smashes it angrily on the floor.*

Dialogue.

MARION: Who are you?

J: I don't know why you doom yourself to this.

MARION: Why are you here?

J: I'm telling them your story.

MARION: One of those newspaper men—

J: I thought a transfer to London meant I'd be covering the complete decline of what remained of the British Empire.

But here we are.

MARION: —And a newspaper man who hasn't sorted out his colonial accent.

J: My accent doesn't need sorting out.

MARION: If you want to be taken seriously by them, I'd recommend a complete annihilation of that twang.

J: Didn't work for you.

MARION: An Australian trying get a scoop.

Thinking your irreverence is a badge of honour.

You're not the first.

You won't get me aiding your cause.

I love Her.

I'm sick of people thinking they can tell my story.

That they know my story. I know my story. She knows my story.

Off you trot.

And my goodness, I never did that. With the cup.

In what world would I smash a perfectly lovely tea cup, given to me by the Queen?

Clean it up.

She clears up the tea party, then goes to set it up again, as if on autopilot.

Narration.

J: Go to London, they say.

It's a rite of passage, they say.

Cover the big stories of global importance.

'No!' says the boss over dinner at the Ivy, after a thirty-hour flight from Adelaide. 'I'm putting you on the royal beat.'

And here I am.

Inside a detached house on a hill in Aberdeen.

Cleaning up after a lonely old Scottish lady in an endless purgatory of tea parties no-one shows up to.

2. A FUN MUMMY AND A FUN PAPA DISCUSS A FUN NANNY, 1931

Narration.

J: The colonisation of the woman you just met?

   It begins decades before.

   1931.

   A time that's positively ancient to us.

   Between two world wars, a mother and a father are deciding who might have the great honour of what we'd call 'babysitting' their two young daughters.

   While they get ready for fun. They're there for fun.

ELIZABETH: I live for fun.

J: No everyday concerns for them.

   No worrying about the rent.

   No worrying about how to feed their family.

   No worrying, really, about anything.

   Can you imagine?

   Just fun.

ELIZABETH: I'm mad for fun!

J: The youngish mother is known for bringing a jolly good time.

   You want to enliven a party? Invite Elizabeth.

   She's married to that rather awkward duke they call 'Bertie', but no-one is perfect.

   And, let's be real, the husband is her ticket.

   It's because of the husband whatever room they sleep in will eventually be pointed out during a historical tour of said house.

   I mean, castle. These are castle people.

   Dialogue.

ELIZABETH: Bertie, did you meet that little nanny Minty brought from Scotland for the summer?

BERTIE: I'd hardly say she's little, Buffy.

ELIZABETH: So you did meet the tall nanny Minty brought from Scotland for the summer?

BERTIE: Very briefly, at elevenses.

ELIZABETH: What did you think of her?

BERTIE: The darnedest thing, Buffy. She drank coffee.

ELIZABETH: And?

BERTIE: Rather modern, don't you think? The drinking of coffee?

ELIZABETH: Bertie.

We need someone with pep and energy.

Perhaps her pep and energy comes from the coffee?

Perhaps we could do with more coffee?

BERTIE: Buffy, you hardly need more pep and energy.

ELIZABETH: She's kindly, but not dull.

I usually find kindly people dreadfully dull.

And she certainly seemed to keep up with the children.

Running after them.

Playing hopscotch.

BERTIE: I do love hopscotch.

ELIZABETH: I know you love hopscotch.

Think of the hopscotch you might play at elevenses.

BERTIE: I'm awfully good at hopscotch.

ELIZABETH: I dare say you'll get even better at hopscotch should we
have a governess who excels in the hopscotch arts.

BERTIE: Quite.

ELIZABETH: Bertie.

I have been rather naughty.

I've already offered her the position!

As we speak, she's on her way from Scotland!

BERTIE: Shouldn't we have her meet Lilibet first? See if they get on?

ELIZABETH: Everyone gets on with Lilibet, Bertie.

She's very mousey, isn't she?

BERTIE: Lilibet's not at all mousey—

ELIZABETH: The tall nanny, Bertie, not Lilibet!

Only the most imbecilic families invite in a beautiful nanny—

BERTIE: Good God, Buffy.

You know how scared I am of nannies.

Their tempers. Their sharp elbows.

ELIZABETH: Minty says she's very discreet.

Keeps oyster.

BERTIE: Jolly good.

ELIZABETH: Minty tried to get her to dish the dirt on the Earl and Countess and she wouldn't—

BERTIE: Perhaps there's no dirt on the Elgins.

ELIZABETH: Bertie.

You know there's a quarry of dirt on the Elgins.

Most likely from a quarry in the Far East they've shipped in under dubious circumstances.

They are naughty.

Bertie.

Bertie!

Are you very pleased?

BERTIE: Yes, Buffy.

ELIZABETH: Are you very pleased I found a young, fun, but not at all beautiful nanny?

BERTIE: No sharp elbows for our girls—

ELIZABETH: If you can't be happy as a little princess, when can you be happy?

The tall nanny.

I can tell already.

She'll be practically perfect in every way.

BERTIE: If you say so.

ELIZABETH: I knew you'd be ecstatically happy!

Now. Let's have some drinky-poos.

She arrives in a few hours.

Let's make sure we're a little fizzy, but not sozzled.

She must know I'm a fun mummy and you're a fun papa.

And we shall all be very happy together for a very long time and—

BERTIE: Buffy?

ELIZABETH: Yes, Bertie?

BERTIE: Before Ainslie shows her to her room?

ELIZABETH: Yes, Bertie?

BERTIE: Check her elbows.

3. MARION PUTS HER SUBSTANTIAL FOOT IN HER SUBSTANTIAL MOUTH, 1931

Narration.

J: At that very moment,

When the Duchess is taking her second cocktail of the day,

Marion Crawford has a bag packed with clothes she's had her mother mend, including a dress that (in the spirit of great heroines and nannies before and after) was crafted out of a long-forgotten curtain.

MARION: What absolute tosh.

J: I'm building a nanny narrative here—

MARION: A dress out of a curtain.

Please.

Have you ever worn a dress made out of a heavy Scottish curtain?

Excellent way to get a rash and a bad back.

J: She's waiting for the train to London.

Marion's what the current parlance might call a 'career girl'.

She wants to have a life before she has a family.

She knows a period of employment with that lot will be excellent for her future prospects.

And afternoon tea anecdotes.

But they're in no way her end game—

MARION: Six months at the most and then I'm back to college.

I'm top of my class.

The professor thinks I've it in me to be a fine English teacher, or even a psychologist for children—'If the usual stuff of a woman's life doesn't get in the way.'

'The usual stuff.' Meaning the birthing of children.

I dream of 'the usual stuff' getting in the way.

I'll have my own children. Lots of them.

It's 1931.

A modern woman doesn't let babies get in the way of her dreams.

She includes them in her dreams.

J: The train speeds out of Dunfermline, a change at Edinburgh.

Across the border into England.

A woman sits across from her.
Warm smile, warm eyes.

Dialogue.

MARION: My mother packed enough curried egg sandwiches to feed the Rangers at half-time.

Would you like one, or five?

The quicker we eat them the better, else the whole carriage will be filled with their sulphuric fumes.

And my cunning plan?

They'll blame us both if you're spied tucking in too.

NANNY: I've never known an opportunity to turn down a curried egg sandwich.

Your mother loves you—

MARION: My mother thinks I'm making the mistake of my life.

NANNY: How so, hen?

MARION: I'm heading to London to be a nanny, just for the summer.

I have a brain.

I won't have it calcifying.

Filling in hours playing doll's houses with five-year-olds. A surrogate mother while their real mother is enjoying the world.

What takes you to London?

NANNY: I'm a nanny.

MARION: Oh!

I do beg your pardon!

Have I put my enormous foot in my very stupid mouth?

NANNY: People often think we're idiots.

Dimwitted child wardens in grey tweed.

MARION: Do you think there's any chance this seat might swallow me up?

Feed me to the tracks below?

I'm doing it for the family.

They'll make for a good story.

Much more exciting than serving tea and sandwiches at the local caff over my holidays.

What is your family like?

NANNY: I've brought up three generations of my family.

Two members of parliament and a leader of the suffragette movement.

MARION: You must be a good nanny!

NANNY: I make them feel loved.

MARION: Love isn't family connections.

Love isn't going to the right schools and universities—

NANNY: Look at the current crop at Westminster.

Winston Churchill. Clement Attlee.

War heroes, public servants.

They had the same nanny!

Guiding them, loving them.

They're fine, upstanding men of service.

Look down the road to Buckingham Palace and the children of King George.

Terrible nanny. Cruel.

And they're a messy lot, hen!

The Prince of Wales does nothing with his life but go to parties and have affairs with married women.

The Duke of York, God bless him, is so damaged they say he cannae speak properly.

No love will do that.

You love a child—they can do anything.

Love creates a sense of self-worth.

Security.

Goodness.

MARION: Do you have your own children?

NANNY: Time got away from me, hen.

MARION: I'm sorry.

NANNY: Wasnae meant to be.

But I've loved my children like they're my children.

The train arrives at London Kings Cross.

MARION: Lovely to blether.

NANNY: A wee addendum to the case of Mr Churchill, hen.

And yes, as well as the odd doll's house fit-out, a nanny can learn and use a word like 'addendum'.

MARION: Forgive me for—

NANNY: His nanny, a Mrs Everest.

When she got ill, he helped nurse her.

He was holding her hand when she died.

MARION: I wish you the same for all you've clearly given your family.

NANNY: And hen: keep everything.

Remember everything.

Write down everything.

I've been living history and it could be the same for you.

I'm glad to see you've already got an excellent carpet bag.

A carpet bag is an essential item for every serious nanny.

MARION: I'm not a serious nanny! I'm a nanny for a summer!

A nanny for a good story—

Narration.

J: Marion gets off the train.

She thinks the old woman has been carpet-bagged by the aristocracy.

MARION: Then I notice all the women getting off the train.

J: She's never seen so much grey tweed.

MARION: Cotton blouses done right to the top.

J: Every skirt hemmed at an appropriate length.

MARION: And so many sensible shoes.

J: These women—

MARION: All nannies.

J: Putting in the hard yards—

MARION: Raising the children—

J: For the top end of town—

MARION: Their work—

J: Means another woman's freedom—

MARION: This Mrs Everest.

When the biographies of Churchill are written, will she be in them?

J: She's not even in the early life section of his 'Wikipedia' page.

MARION: I will not be a dried-up old spinster, faceless in this mass of returning grey tweed.

Bringing up other people's babies.

Forgotten.

J: I hate to be that guy, but get yourself ready.
You'll be in sensible shoes in no time.

MARION: I will not.

J: You won't be completely forgotten though—

MARION: Encyclopedia Britannica?
Marion Kirk Crawford. Born 1909, Gatehead Scotland.
An educational pioneer who was also able to raise six of her own children, two of whom were prime ministers of—

J: Have you ever heard of Maria Von Trapp? Mary Poppins?

MARION: What sort of a name is Poppins?
And what the devil is a Wikipedia page?

4. LOVE AT FIRST NEIGH, 1931

Narration.

J: It's late when she arrives at One-Four-Five Piccadilly.

The quaint family town house of the Yorks.

MARION: If you can call a twenty-five bedroom mansion in the middle of London 'quaint'.

J: She's welcomed not by her new employers, so keen to greet her as the 'fun' parents, but by Ainslie, their butler—

Dialogue.

AINSLIE: Miss Crawford.

Their Royal Highnesses are still out 'on the town'. They apologise.

They meant to be here to greet you,

But the cocktails are flowing rather freely tonight at the Astor Club.

And one can't possibly be home when the cocktails are flowing rather freely at the Astor Club.

You'll meet the Duchess in the morning,

To discuss the particulars of your post with the princesses.

MARION: What time should I be ready?

AINSLIE: How should I know?

I'm their butler, not yours.

MARION: Oh, I beg your pardon, I—

AINSLIE: Your guess is as good as mine and it directly corresponds—

With how many cocktails have flown freely at the Astor Club.

I believe the Princess Elizabeth is still awake.

Her room is right beside yours.

MARION: A five-year-old?

Still up at ten-thirty at night?

I never—

AINSLIE: Well, she's 'never' either.

Up the stairs, turn left, go to the end of the corridor where you'll find the nursery.

No doubt you'll hear it first.

MARION: Hear it?

AINSLIE: Horses, Miss Crawford.

MARION: There are horses in the house?

AINSLIE: Make your way towards the neighing, Miss Crawford.

You'll get used to making your way towards the neighing.

> *Off to the nursery* MARION *goes. It doesn't take long for her to hear the sound of a little girl neighing. Immediately,* MARION *is playful.*

> *She knocks a special knock. There's a neigh that almost sounds like 'Come in!'*

MARION: Excuse me, but why is there a horse running rampant through a very lovely house so late in the night?

Shouldn't such a beautiful, majestic, brilliant animal be in a stable?

Tucked inside her blanket? On fresh hay?

Dreaming of eating chocolate-covered tadpoles?

LILIBET: Horses don't eat chocolate-covered tadpoles!

MARION: Why ever not? They're completely scrumptious!

LILIBET: I should think it's very hard to get a chocolate on a tadpole.

MARION: If horses can talk, tadpoles can surely be covered in chocolate.

LILIBET: Horses can't talk—

MARION: What do you mean? You're talking to me now!

LILIBET: I'm not a horse, madam, can't you see? I'm a girl!

I'm actually Lilibet and I'm very glad to meet you.

MARION: I'm Miss—

LILIBET: Crawford, yes. I know.

How many horses do you have?

MARION: I'm afraid my horse exists only in my imagination.

He's stabled inside this book. Do you know him?

LILIBET: He looks very beautiful. What's his name?

MARION: Black Beauty. And I brought this special copy for you.

LILIBET: How wonderful!

I've never read a chapter book—

MARION: Something tells me you'll take to them like a gelding to his morning hay—

LILIBET: I do love geldings.

You do know, of course, they're the sweetest of all horses.

MARION: I can't wait for you to teach me all about them.

For now though, Lilibet, I think it's time for you to get to your bed.

LILIBET: You're quite right.

It's extremely late.

Will you help me put the horses in their stables?

LILIBET *takes* MARION *by the hand to the tiny toy horses.*

Narration.

MARION: Her tiny hand.

It's warm and soft.

It fits perfectly in mine.

Immediately.

I can't quite describe it.

I'm home with this child.

5. THE RULES OF ENGAGEMENT, 1931

It's 11.30 a.m. ELIZABETH *is drinking down a hangover salve.*
Dialogue.

ELIZABETH: My word, Ainslie, this is bloody awful.

AINSLIE: Apparently it does the trick a mere ten seconds after the last sip is supped.

All the rage in America.

ELIZABETH: What did you say is in it?

AINSLIE: Worcestershire sauce, vinegar, salt, Tabasco sauce, black pepper … and a raw egg from the Buckingham Palace chicken coop.

It's called a 'prairie oyster'.

She finishes the drink. They count the ten seconds.

ELIZABETH: That's rather a miracle, Ainslie!

I don't feel the least bit hung!

You do look after me, dear old fruit!

Ainslie, bring me the new builder of our girls' character!

Bring me Miss Crawford!

AINSLIE: She's waiting right outside the door.

Since six-thirty.

ELIZABETH: She has her breakfast at six-thirty?

AINSLIE: Scottish.

ELIZABETH: My word, Ainslie.

AINSLIE: The Duke does say, Ma'am, 'The world belongs to those who wake up early.'

ELIZABETH: He does, Ainslie.

But you mustn't give the Duke credit for such wisdom.

I'm sure you'll find it was Wordsworth, or Keats, or someone equally as dreary, who'd never had a moment's fun in all their lives.

Not like you or I, Ainslie.

AINSLIE: Quite, Ma'am.

ELIZABETH: Now then, let's have this new nanny!

MARION *enters, curtsies.*

MARION: Good morning, Your Royal Highness.

ELIZABETH: Ah, Miss Crawford.

Let me guess how you like your tea?

And then you shall guess how I like mine, and we shall be acquainted properly from that moment on.

You're from Dunfermline?

MARION: Mostly. Born in Ayrshire.

Lived there for the first few years of my life—

ELIZABETH: That changes things.

MARION: It does?

ELIZABETH: The east and west coasts of Scotland might as well be different countries.

Certainly when it comes to one's tea preferences.

Those on the west coast don't allow themselves as many pleasures.

Therefore, I'd wager that, and your slim figure, means it's rare that sugar illuminates the tea you drink.

MARION: I'm sorry to tell you, Ma'am, you're quite mistaken.

I like the heftiest amount of sugar available to me.

What I think I might get away with in the company I'm keeping.

With my mother, for instance, just the one. I'd rather evade her Presbyterian judgement.

But with you?

I know you hail from the east coast of Scotland.

You have a wee glint in your eye that suggests you're open to an excess of sugar.

If we'd known each other longer, I'd be going for three … or even four!

Yet, I'll protect my reputation upon first getting to know each other: just two please.

ELIZABETH: Miss Crawford. Are you wild?

MARION: Wildly sweet of tooth.

ELIZABETH: I knew you were right for the girls!

I knew it!

MARION: Because I have a weakness for sweetness?

ELIZABETH: A weakness for sweetness suggests you still have the child in you.

MARION: Do you have a weakness for sweetness?

ELIZABETH: Miss Crawford.

It's not proper to ask a member of the Royal Family any personal questions.

MARION: I beg your pardon.

ELIZABETH: It's quite all right.

I think you and I will scrap that rule as we're to be joined in the family endeavour of bringing up happy little girls.

Look at me, Miss Crawford.

Does it look like I have a weakness for sweetness?

You don't have to answer that, but suffice to say I'm most aware that my brother-in-law David and his waifish paramours call me 'Cookie'.

Apparently, Miss Crawford, because I am as round as an American chocolate chip cookie.

Now then!

We must get to the bitty nitty pretty gritty of what we need from you—

MARION: Yes, Ma'am.

ELIZABETH: I suspect Lilibet's fate will include some nice country chap.

You know the type—red-faced and slightly gouty.

She'll have a few children, breed some race horses and live a thoroughly delightful life.

Margo's still a baby, she's a little wild, so who knows?

What I'm saying, Miss Crawford, is please don't feel too much pressure about their academic education.

As long as they can read, write, are happy and thought of as pleasant people—that's all their father and I care about.

MARION: Ma'am?

ELIZABETH: Yes, Miss Crawford.

MARION: I think you might have chosen the wrong person.

I believe girls need to be educated for the future of this world.

To make it better.

They can't do a worse job than men have over the last thousand years or so.

ELIZABETH: Miss Crawford.

MARION: Yes, Ma'am.

ELIZABETH: These men of which you speak—

MARION: Yes, Ma'am.

ELIZABETH: You do realise that many of them have sipped brandy in this very room?

MARION: Yes, Ma'am.

I want more ladies making more decisions for our world.

A good education is key to that.

ELIZABETH: I see.

MARION: I suppose then I'll be heading back to the station, Ma'am.

Thank you for the splendid night in your lovely home—

ELIZABETH: Miss Crawford, you'll not be going anywhere.

I like your spirit!

We could do with a nanny in this family who doesn't need a feather duster taken to her brain.

Teach them what you like, but I keep a happy house, so, as long as the girls are pleasant, do fill their heads with anything you like!

Except Marxism.

MARION: I'd venture—the girls should learn about Marxism, if they're put upon to make a case against it.

ELIZABETH: Glorious.

And one more thing, dear Miss Crawford.

I can tell you're an absolute darling, but it's most important when you go home to Scotland:

You must keep oyster.

MARION: 'Oyster', Ma'am?

ELIZABETH: You'll find everyone will want to know about us.

Whether the girls behave (they do), whether Bertie and I bicker (we do), whether the Prince of Wales is an attentive uncle (he is, surprisingly).

I don't need to tell you how the newspapers survive—on us being very good stories.

But these stories must not come from you.

If one must share a story from time to time (and, Miss Crawford, who among us doesn't like an indiscreet little chitty chat?), share with the other staff.

You'll find particularly receptive ears in Ainslie.

Just keep oyster everywhere else.

Oyster.

Snapped shut.

MARION: You won't need to worry about me and gossip, Ma'am.

People don't tend to gossip with me.

I've always thought maybe it's to do with my posture.

ELIZABETH: You have excellent posture.

MARION: Aye—people who gossip tend to have less erect posture.

All the leaning in to hear the secrets, et cetera.

ELIZABETH: Ha! How very clever of you, Miss Crawford.

I'm doing an inventory right this moment of all my friends who love some salacious chittity and you're quite right!

None of them are erect of posture.

Goodness me!

I'll have to start standing up taller!

ELIZABETH *rings the bell, their time together is over.*

Thank you, Miss Crawford.

Of course we'll need another name for you—

MARION: I'm not really one for silly names—

ELIZABETH: Crawfo? Crawfiddley-poo? Crawfie?

Crawfie!

Oh yes!

I think 'Crawfie' suits you very well.

MARION: Crawfie?

In the classroom, with the girls, I'm not sure it sets the right tone—

ELIZABETH: And Crawfie—that accent won't do if you stay on with us.

Of course I adore the lilt of a Scot nearby—actually makes me frightfully homesick for my own dear nanny, would you believe?

But we can't have the princesses—

MARION: I've college to be going back to when spring comes.

It's very much in Scotland.

ELIZABETH: Yes, yes, Crawfie.

But you'll fall in love with us. Everyone does. It becomes completely impossible to leave us!

Ask Ainslie.

Isn't it so, Ainslie?

Isn't it simply completely impossible to leave us?

AINSLIE: Yes, Ma'am.

Impossible.

ELIZABETH: And you'll never guess where Ainslie is originally from.

He's done a beautiful job with his accent. Beautiful!

Go on, Ainslie.

Be a peach and do some of your old accent?

AINSLIE: I'm afraid I've quite forgotten, Ma'am.

ELIZABETH: Poppycock, dear Ainslie.

Please, Ainslie.

It's so delightful when you do it.

What if I do it?

I'm a really rather excellent mimic, aren't I Ainslie?

AINSLIE: Yes you are, Ma'am.

ELIZABETH: [*in Cockney*] Ainslie is from the East End of London, innit!

I'm off to find me old pot and pan!

ELIZABETH *exits, laughing.*

AINSLIE: Excellent, Ma'am!

MARION: How long have you been here, Ainslie?

AINSLIE: Seventeen years, Miss Crawford.

Stay here seventeen years and you can erase that very essence of yourself too.

6. LEARNING TO BE A NORMAL, 1931–1935

Narration.

MARION: If it was up to Lilibet, all our work in the schoolroom would be—
LILIBET: Black Beauty—
MARION: Black Beauty's life of service—
LILIBET: Black Beauty's struggles! The life of Anna Sewell!
MARION: Anna Sewell is the author of *Black Beauty*.

> She also loves to hear tales of people outside the castles.
>
> Their 'normal' lives.
>
> The people who gather in front of her grandpapa's palace to wave on special days.
>
> I decide to do something royal children haven't been able to do before.
>
> I take her out into the world.

Dialogue.

LILIBET: Crawfie, I have my purse ready, my coins ready, are we really going on 'the tube'?
MARION: Yes darling.
LILIBET: Grandpapa's face is on this coin!

> And this one!
>
> And this one!
>
> Oh Crawfie, you really do make everything ever so special.

MARION: Darling, I didn't do a thing.

> Grandpapa's face is on all the coins.
>
> That's one of the things that goes with being a king.

LILIBET: My word!

> Can I pay for my ticket myself?

MARION: I won't be doing it for you.

> We go down into the tube station.

And they're there, at the tube.

> We're at the ticket office. And—
>
> Do you remember what to say, Lilibet?

LILIBET: I'd like a return trip to Tottenham Court Road, please.

MARION: Perfect.

LILIBET: Do I hand over my actual coins, Crawfie?

Actual money?

MARION: Yes, count it out.

LILIBET: I don't have the correct amount!

MARION: Wait to get some money back, dear. 'Change', we call it.
''Ere's your change, little madam!'

LILIBET: 'Change'.

And now what, Crawfie?

MARION: We're going through the ticket turnstile and down, down into the Underground.

LILIBET: It's a very long escalator!

MARION: And now we're off the escalator and we're on the train—

LILIBET: We'll sit with all the people?

MARION: If there's room.

LILIBET: Might we have to stand?

MARION: We might.

LILIBET: Marvellous! And then?

MARION: We're standing on the tube. It shoots off to its next destination.
We hold tightly to the hand railings.

LILIBET: Look, Crawfie!

Everyone is reading their papers.

That man is doing a crossword.

Does that lady have kippers on her sandwich? Kippers?!

MARION: Shhh hen.

LILIBET: Can you imagine how wonderful it would be to take the tube every day?

MARION: Most are on the tube to get to their jobs.

LILIBET: They look so grumpy!

MARION: Most people have a job they don't like!

LILIBET: Why would anyone do a job if they don't like it?

How very peculiar!

That lady has very red hands, Crawfie. Does she need some ointment? Can we give her some ointment?

Do you think she'd like the skills for a different job?

MARION: I expect she's not thinking much further than cooking dinner tonight for her family—

LILIBET: She doesn't have a cook?

MARION: No, darling. Most people don't have a cook.

LILIBET: Why don't most people have a cook?

MARION: It comes down to those coins in your purse. And time, Lilibet.

LILIBET: Do Mummy and Papa have lots of coins and time?

MARION: They do.

LILIBET: Why?

MARION: I suppose they're very lucky. And so are you.

LILIBET: And the lady with the red hands? She doesn't have lots of coins and time? She's not very lucky?

MARION: She's a working person. Without working people, this train wouldn't work.

London wouldn't even exist.

You must always treat these people with courtesy and respect.

And let people tell you who they are before you decide for yourself what someone's story is.

LILIBET: Yes, Crawfie.

Could we ask that man with one arm to tell us his story?

MARION: Off we get!

> MARION *gets* LILIBET *off the train.*

Later that night …

LILIBET: Crawfie, might I come in?

MARION: Only if you know the special knock!

> *KNOCK KNOCK KNOCK KNOCK. A special, rhythmic knock.*

LILIBET: I think today was the greatest day of my life.

I've realised these 'working people' are just like Black Beauty! She's a working horse!

What was your favourite part of the day?

MARION: When you left your teapot on the counter and—

LILIBET: That lady with the purple face roused on me?

Oh please, Crawfie, please do again how she roused on me!

MARION: 'Oy! Little Lady! This tea not good enough for your tray? You think youse the Queen of Sheba or somethin'?'

LILIBET: I'd like to be a working person when I grow up, Crawfie.

MARION: Let's get you ready!

You'll need 'faith, courage and a quiet heart'.

LILIBET: 'Faith, courage and a quiet heart.'

Crawfie. Why should my heart have to be quiet?

MARION: Sometimes when our hearts are loud, we forget others are just trying to do their best. Always assume the best of people, Lilibet. You'll be disappointed from time to time, but mostly you'll be rewarded with friendship and love.

Now off to your stable for the night, please, Black Beauty!

LILIBET: Crawfie. Can you keep my ticket safe? I want to remember this day forever.

Narration.

MARION: The ticket stubs go into the carpet bag.

I go to bed heart-warm.

Teaching this receptive, curious little girl every day is as heart-filling as I imagined the Glasgow Tenements would be.

J: As much as Crawfie loves Lilibet, she knows in the back of her mind that life at One-Four-Five Piccadilly isn't her endgame.

She still has her plans, her dreams, and they don't involve times tables with a princess.

They're getting mistier, but they're there—

MARION: How, pray tell, would you know anything about what's misty or clear or hypercolour in the back of my mind?

J: Everything is about to change because one day on the train between Kings Cross and Aberdeen, Marion Crawford meets George Buthlay—

7. A SCOTTISH ROMANCE WITH A PERSON OF FUN, 1935

Narration.

MARION: George Buthlay!

J: George Buthlay.

> Marion Crawford gets two holidays a year.
> In the summer, when she goes to her mother who's now in a council house in Aberdeen.

MARION: And at Christmas.

> When I go to my mother who's now in a council house in Aberdeen.
> Are you getting how exciting my life is?
> How connected it is with the real world?
> It's all nine-year-old Lilibet and four-year-old Margo.
> And Ainslie the butler.
> Who I think is rather impressed at how quickly I've taken to Englishing up my 'Rains in Spain Fall Mainly in the Plains'.

J: She's been with the Yorks for four years.

> Turns out it's hard to leave palaces for an attic room in a council house in Aberdeen with Mother.

MARION: As the train winds itself up to Scotland and the air gets cleaner, and the hills get greener, and the sea gets clearer—

J: She begins to unwind.

MARION: My accent 'regresses' as my elocution teacher, Ainslie, would say.

> It becomes more Scottish.
> My life is fine, isn't it?
> Life is rather exciting with Lilibet and the Yorks.
> I'm fine not returning to college.
> Life is rather exciting with Lilibet and the Yorks.

> MARION *is on the train. Next to* GEORGE *Buthlay.*

I realise I'm sitting next to a man.

> A man who's very handsome.
> A man who smiles at me with what they call—
> A wee sparkle in his eye.

Dialogue.

GEORGE: Are you really going to read that book for a second time when you could be talking to me?

MARION: You've had from London to … Darlington to talk to me.

GEORGE: I had to come up with just the right line.

MARION: And you think you did?

GEORGE: I have your attention, don't I?

MARION: Only because I know where Mr Dickens and Tiny Tim are taking me.

I've no idea where you'll take me.

GEORGE: Your ticket says Aberdeen.

How about the Esplanade?

MARION: To do what?

GEORGE: A fish supper drenched in finest vinegar?

A stroll along the windy shore?

MARION: Scottish men.

You know how to woo a lady.

GEORGE: Aye, we do!

With tender, soft, batter-covered haddock, and windchill from the waves to make you so cold you've no choice but to seek refuge in my fiddle-playing arms.

MARION: That's very brash.

GEORGE: Living through a Great War will do that to a man.

What's the point of waiting about?

MARION: Indeed.

GEORGE: And why is a bonnie girl like you on a train from London in grey tweed?

Beautiful hair up so tight?

No rings? No weeuns?

MARION: I have a busy life in London. Not much time for romance—

GEORGE: Or weeuns?

MARION: It's all weeuns.

Narration.

I tell him about Lilibet and Margo, without telling him about Lilibet and Margo.

I've learned to keep oyster with anyone new.

Until I get to know them.
And I get to know George Buthlay.
He plays fiddle in bands all over Aberdeen.
Every night we're dancing somewhere new!
He's not perfect—

GEORGE: I love a wee dram or ten on a Saturday night—

MARION: He's divorced with a son in Fyfe—

GEORGE: Isn't life too short to be in an unhappy marriage?

MARION: He's never quite settled into a profession—

GEORGE: I've had an adventurous life—

MARION: I love that he's had an adventurous life—

GEORGE: I've tried it all—

MARION: I love that he's tried it all—

He's been a fisherman—

GEORGE: A soldier—

MARION: A union organiser—

GEORGE: A musician—

MARION: And now he's in banking.

He has a big life!

GEORGE: A big life—

And in my spare time I help the laddies hand out for the Scottish
Party.

Beat.

Dialogue.

MARION: Oh.

GEORGE: 'Oh?' You don't believe in an independent Scotland?

Beat.

Don't tell me my perfect lass is all about King and Country?
Has she spent too much time in England?
Has she let the creamy Victorian sponge cake go to her head?

MARION: George.

My job.

The girls.

The girls are the King's grandchildren.

My pay comes each month from the Royal Family.

The rather enormous house I live in at Piccadilly?
It's with the Duke and Duchess of York.

> *Beat.*

GEORGE: Do you plan on forsaking the pleasures of Aberdeen to be in London forever?

MARION: I never planned to be there more than six months.

GEORGE: Do they know how special you are?

MARION: George.

GEORGE: Do they?

MARION: They're my family now George.

GEORGE: Really?

That lot can treat their nanny like family?

MARION: I'm their governess.

GEORGE: A governess is just a servant in grey tweed.

MARION: I'm teaching the girls how to be in the world.

> *Beat.*

GEORGE: Lucky bloody English weeuns!

MARION: Will you still take me dancing? To the sea for haddock?

GEORGE: Now I know you're for King and Country?

MARION: They're not so bad, George.

GEORGE: It'll take a lot more than being a royalist to get rid of me!

MARION: I'm not really a royalist. I'm not not a royalist. But—

GEORGE: You must have quite the reputation. Quite the connections.

I've loved you since I saw that beautiful calf muscle, underneath a grey tweed skirt on the train to Aberdeen.

Marion Kirk Crawford.

You know I'm a man of action.

Someone who won't let even the prettiest highland grasses grow under my feet.

With that in mind—will you be my wife?

MARION: I will!

GEORGE: Now?

MARION: I want a wedding!

A beautiful, Scottish wedding at the Dunfermline Cathedral!

White dress, a lace veil—

GEORGE: Little princesses as flower girls?

MARION: How will your Scottish Party friends feel about it?

GEORGE: They'll probably want their picture taken with them!
Do you think I could get my picture taken with them?
You'll come back to Scotland to live.
I'll keep making my way up in the bank.
We'll get a detached house on a hill in Aberdeen and we'll have weeuns of our own.

MARION: Weeuns of our own?

GEORGE: It would be an absolute crime not to reproduce that brilliant brain, that beautiful face at least ten times over!
Imagine the ten bairns we'd make!

MARION: Your sparkle!

GEORGE: Your nose!

MARION: Your lips!

GEORGE: Your goodness!

MARION: Your fun!
My own baby.
Our own baby.

GEORGE: A family of your own.

MARION: A family of our own.

8. *A ROYAL SUMMONS ONE CAN'T REFUSE, 1936*

Narration.

ELIZABETH: Crawfie!

Back to London immediately!

Of course by now you've heard the news and there's a first-class ticket in your name at Aberdeen Station.

Bid goodbye to your mother!

Directly!

Be of service to us! And your new King!

Lilibet is quite beside herself to have lost her dear grandpapa. She really thought him a darling old man, which he absolutely was not. She's absolutely fixated on what happens to the coins now. Of course, he tortured poor dear Bertie, who's bizarrely, desperately sad!

I can't deal with either of them and their ridiculous grief!

London is beyond miserable. Streets are quiet in a way that's almost unseemly. No fun at all. Which I suppose is to be expected until the dear old King is buried.

Hurry back, dear Crawfie, we need you desperately!

The King is dead. God save the King (and Mrs Simpson)!

9. ALL LIVES CHANGE AT THE SWIMMING POOL, 1936

Narration.

J: As you may have guessed, there won't be a summer wedding for Marion Kirk Crawford.

Doesn't stop George from trying to convince her to come back to Aberdeen—

MARION: I want to be with him.

You would too if you knew the smell of his coat after a walk in the rain.

J: She gathers up her courage.

Gets ready to give her notice.

MARION: Again and again I request an audience with the Duchess.

A private audience.

J: Woman to woman.

To tell her of her romance. Her plans for bairns with George Buthlay.

MARION: She'll be needing to find someone to take my place.

I have my own life to live.

J: Good luck.

There's drama in the air at One-Four-Five Piccadilly.

Lots of comings and goings.

MARION: I can't get her alone.

She brings the Duke to the Bath Club, where Lilibet is doing the final test for her lifesaving medal.

> MARION, ELIZABETH *and* BERTIE *are all watching* LILIBET *in the pool.* BERTIE *is very anxious and whatever he does have to say should show his stammer in full flight.*
>
> *Dialogue.*

ELIZABETH: Go, Lilibet!

MARION: Good work, Lilibet!

ELIZABETH: Isn't she doing well? Bertie. Isn't she doing well?

BERTIE: She's doing well Buffy.

ELIZABETH: I had no idea she was such a little brown trout!

I almost want to get my line and fish her out!

She looks so delicious!

Get Cook to roast her!

Serve her perfect little body up with roast potatoes!

MARION: I can't tell you how much she's loved being with the other girls.

Swimming with them. Being an ordinary girl.

BERTIE: 'Ordinary'. Ha!

ELIZABETH: Now, Bertie—

BERTIE: She'd bloody well better enjoy it—

ELIZABETH: Now, Bertie—

BERTIE: Damn that bastard and his double divorcee!

ELIZABETH: Do you need to go and sit in the sauna and calm down?

MARION: Is this our audience, Ma'am?

ELIZABETH: Whatever do you mean, Crawfie?

MARION: I have something to discuss with you—

ELIZABETH: Dear Crawfie, I'm afraid whatever it is will need to wait—

BERTIE: It's bloody happened.

What we worried would happen.

It's happened.

ELIZABETH: Of course what Bertie is trying to say is that you're no longer the governess to little princesses who will grow up to have lovely lives as wives of earls.

You're now governess to the future Queen of England.

BERTIE: I'm fur—

ELIZABETH: As you can see, Bertie is furious.

I am too.

For God's sake.

Is David still a child in the first flush of puberty?

'Love'?

When has anyone in this family cared for 'love'?

BERTIE: Buffy—

ELIZABETH: Think about what he's done.

Think.

For a moment.

Our lovely life. Our lovely home.

We have to leave it to live in that mausoleum they call Buckingham Palace!

It's beyond ghastly. Mice everywhere!

And it's freezing. Why is it freezing?

How have they not sorted that out yet?

Go, Lilibet!

Poor Lilibet. Poor dear Lilibet.

'Love'. How absolutely juvenile. Ridiculous.

BERTIE: It's very important now, Crawfie—

MARION: Yes Sir?

BERTIE: Lilibet's education is more rigorous in affairs of state. History. Geography.

ELIZABETH: What sort of little girl wants to learn Geography?! The horror!

Curse Mrs Simpson with her horrid little waist.

I've never trusted anyone with a tiny waist, never!

Hungry people simply cannot think in a reasonable manner!

And those revolting moles on her very masculine face—

BERTIE: Buffy!

ELIZABETH: It's true! Don't you think it's true, Crawfie? Very masculine face.

BERTIE: You don't have to answer, Crawfie—

ELIZABETH: Bertie! Go home!

If you can't say something nasty about Mrs Simpson, you shouldn't say anything at all!

Exit, the soon-to-be King.

MARION: I haven't been close enough to her face. To see if it's masculine or not.

ELIZABETH: Take my word for it. It's very masculine.

Good show old trout!

First person in this family to earn a certificate through actual work.

Beat.

Tell her tonight, would you, Crawfie?

MARION: You want me to tell her?

ELIZABETH: We're having new portraits done tomorrow and she can't be looking befuddled.

MARION: Forgive me, Ma'am, but this is an enormous life event.
　　　It's something that should come from her mother.
ELIZABETH: You're better with her over things like this.
MARION: I'm not you.
ELIZABETH: She gets one good cry over this.
　　　I'm not allowing any more than that from any of us.
　　　On with it.

> *Exit, the soon-to-be Queen.*
>
> *Edward VIII's abdication speech plays.*
>
> *Narration.*

J: Marion sends her engagement ring back to Scotland.
　　　Leaving Lilibet now isn't an option.
　　　She doesn't expect someone like George to wait for her.
　　　She's been with the Yorks so long now she doesn't even think to ask herself why their responsibilities are of more importance than her dreams.
MARION: Maybe this life is a fine one? An important one?
　　　These are important people and I'm important to them.

10. ROYAL SHOOTING LESSONS, 1939

Narration.

J: Time, as it loves to, marches. And marches. And marches. And marches.

And it looks as though marching is about to come back into fashion.

> ELIZABETH *is at the back of Buckingham Palace. She's methodically checking and loading a gun. Taking aim and shooting rats in the garden. She's loving it. She also has a hip flask, which she'll take a swig or two from during this conversation.*

> MARION *approaches her hesitantly.*

> *Dialogue.*

MARION: Ah, Ma'am?

ELIZABETH: Jolly good. Crawfie.

Be a peach and pass me that box of bullets?

I've always rather loved shooting.

Do you shoot, Crawfie?

MARION: I don't like guns one wee bit.

> *Bang!*

ELIZABETH: Here. Have a go.

Terrible lot of rats out here near the horse feed.

Excellent fun.

> *Bang!*

Got it! I won't have any bloody Nazis coming near us without a fight.

> ELIZABETH *has guns in her pockets. And a small one in her bra.*

I'm afraid Mr Atlee hasn't been at all successful with appeasement. That ghastly Hitler is a rather determined little chap.

> *Bang!*

The Foreign Office want us to take the girls to Canada.

Hide in a house in Saskatchewan.

A place famous for fat salmon and three black bears to every human.

MARION: Lilibet loves salmon.

ELIZABETH: Who doesn't love salmon?

MARION: I'll be getting back to Scotland then.

I can't leave Mother alone if there's another war.

Beat.

ELIZABETH: There's no way the girls are going to Canada.

The children won't go without me.

I won't leave the King.

And the King will never leave.

We'll be needing all hands on deck, Crawfie.

Well, your hands.

And not technically on a deck.

We'll be sending you and the girls to Windsor Castle.

Beat.

MARION: I've been here for eight years and four months, Ma'am.

ELIZABETH: Are we keeping you from something?

A grand romance with a Hebridean crofter?

MARION: It's been three years since the abdication.

I've been thinking about going home.

Having a life of my own.

ELIZABETH: This is your home.

MARION: I always thought I'd have my own children.

ELIZABETH: Are you mad, Crawfie?

Dreadful time for such things.

Bang!

MARION: The threat of war makes you think about what's important—

ELIZABETH: Your mother will be fine.

She's in Scotland.

No-one cares about Scotland.

Here, take one of these—

MARION: No thank you, Ma'am.

ELIZABETH: Take it. Now look over there. If you see a rat trying to run away—

> *Bang!*

Bertie and I will have to be here in London.
> We will, Crawfie. We won't be able to leave.
> We can't have the girls here.
> We've already heard about two kidnapping plots. Two!
> They need to be in Windsor with someone we can trust.
> Who loves them like we do.
> And that's you.

> *Beat.*

We also need someone who's a good shot.

So maybe that's not you, Crawfie, if you're not willing—if you're not hungering—to shoot some Nazis.

They really do need a governess who's happy to shoot a Nazi or two.

> MARION *takes one of the guns from* ELIZABETH, *looks for a rat, aims and shoots.*

You never met my dear mother, Crawfie. She lived for us. She was a woman who made everything magical. By the announcement of Armistice, she'd lost three of her children. You never met her because she barely got out of bed from then until she died.

> Lilibet and Margo, Crawfie.
> They are my life.
> They are what I live for.
> And I need you to know this, Crawfie.
> Nothing must happen to them.
> I don't much like being in bed.

> *Beat.*

The war will start and the war will end.

And then you can go back to your beloved Scotland if you choose.

And live an incredibly dull, miserable, grey, sad life in Aberdeen or Dunfermline or wherever you choose without us.

And you'll miss us, and we'll miss you.

Bang!

The bang turns into a soundscape of war. Bomb whistles ... pauses ... BOMB! Rubble. And repeat. Mixed in with music if it works. 'You'll Never Know' by Vera Lynn is a goodie. Under no circumstances use 'We'll Meet Again'.

11. A WAR ON ITS WAY AND WAR MONTAGE—1939–1945
A.

Narration.

MARION: It's a marvel we haven't been bombarded at Windsor. It's been seven days since the last air raid and the girls haven't been outside.

Lilibet's been begging to see her pony.

We set out into the Great Park—the sunshine is blinding us.

She's traipsing ahead of me in the thick pine forest when THUD.

It can't be more than five yards behind me.

It's a paratrooper. A German paratrooper.

He looks at me. His eyes are as scared as I feel.

He's tangled. He can't get to me. He can't get to her.

Can he get to his gun?

'Run, Lilibet!'

Oh Christ, why did I bring her out here? Why did I shout her name? Stupid! Stupid! Stupid!

I run to catch up to her and I don't know where the strength is coming from but I pick her up and run like I'm the captain of the English Rugby team—

BANG.

A gunshot!

It doesn't get us. I look back to see the paratrooper. He's dead. By his own hand.

We're safe.

I take her little hand in mine. It's warm and soft.

Somehow we're safe.

B.

Dialogue.

AINSLIE: Ma'am. Might I ask for a day or two off?

ELIZABETH: Is something the matter?

AINSLIE: It's my sister, Ma'am. And her husband.

Their home was bombed.

ELIZABETH: Oh. Ainslie, I'm so sorry.

Are they all right?

AINSLIE: They're not, Ma'am, but my nephew is.

I need to go there and work out some accommodations for him.

ELIZABETH: You shall take him to Windsor.

AINSLIE: I couldn't—

ELIZABETH: He'll be safe there. How old is he, Ainslie?

AINSLIE: Fifteen, Ma'am.

ELIZABETH: He shall have a house and a job and I won't hear of it again.

I look forward to meeting him when we next visit the girls.

AINSLIE: Thank you, Ma'am. Thank you.

C.

Narration.

ELIZABETH: It's a quarter to eleven and I'm doing my very best to dislodge a rather stubborn eyelash from Bertie's eye when the unmistakable whirr of the Luftwaffe can be heard.

It's rushing up The Mall towards Buckingham Palace. We've long expected this, but they've yet to pull off.

Before I can even say 'Bloody Germans!', I hear the scream of a bomb, then silence, chilling silence. Then BOOM!

I've got Bertie under a desk while everything around us shatters. Thank Christ we weren't at the window.

I tap my pocket to make sure I've got my pistol.

It's the first of twelve times we're bombed.

It's terrifying and we have to pretend it's not. We have to keep calm and carry on even though our home is rubble and I've no idea if I'll see my children again.

D.

Dialogue.

LILIBET: I don't see why I have to give a speech.

MARION: We'll practise once more and then have a rest.

LILIBET: 'All of us children who are still at home.' Crawfie, we're not at home.

MARION: You're in England. You're at Windsor. That's a home. You should be grateful, Lilibet. Children listening tonight—some have had to go to Canada! To Australia!

LILIBET: I want to be at home in London with Mummy and Papa.

'We are full of cheerfulness and courage.'

That's a lie. We're bored and scared.

MARION: Where's your faith?

LILIBET: Don't you dare start with that 'quiet heart' right now, Crawfie.

I've had quite enough of your 'quiet heart'.

MARION: Lilibet! You won't speak to me like that.

LILIBET: I don't want to give a speech pretending all is well when I'm far away from my mummy when everyone is trying to kill her!

I'd like to see you try and give a speech under those circumstances. How would you like to be away from your mummy?

> LILIBET *scrunches up her script and exits.* MARION *puts the script in her carpet bag.*

MARION: I am, Lilibet.

E.

Narration.

ELIZABETH: The Polish Royal Family are down the road at Claridges. Some of the Greeks are up the hallway in what remains of the Palace. The Czechs, we found them a place in Putney.

King Leopold of Belgium, lovely chap, decided to stay on when they surrendered to the Nazis. He's apparently in some awful camp now. No-one knows if he's alive or dead.

Princess Juliana and Prince Bernhard from the Netherlands— they arrived in England yesterday. With a box. Just one box. No-one helping them with the box. Juliana at one end, Bernhard at the other.

Inside the box? Princess Irene, their daughter.

Good God. What if that were us?

F.

The war has ended. The sound design changes to include some of Churchill's VE Day Speech.

'The German War is therefore at an end. We may allow ourselves a brief moment of rejoicing. But let us not forget the toils and efforts that lie ahead. Advance Britannia. Long live the cause. God save the King.'

MARION, LILIBET *and* ELIZABETH *stand in a shell-shocked row.*

Dialogue.

LILIBET: What happens now?

ELIZABETH: We do everything to make sure it doesn't happen again.

MARION: Shall we celebrate first?

ELIZABETH: I'm not sure my nerves will ever calm enough to celebrate anything ever again.

LILIBET: I'd like to go into the crowds.

ELIZABETH: Whatever for?

LILIBET: We've been cooped up for six years, Mummy.

I'm ready to smell the smokey London air.

I'm ready to dance in the street and drink beer.

I can fix a truck and cook a meal on a campfire I've built myself.

I am not going back to life before, Mummy.

I'm going to be part of the world.

MARION: Let's all go together, Ma'am.

Pop our scarves on.

Have some fun!

ELIZABETH: You two head off.

I'd rather like to go to bed for a week or two.

LILIBET *exits to get ready.*

Crawfie?

MARION: Yes, Ma'am?

ELIZABETH: Job well done indeed.

She's a fine young woman.

The King and I thank you.

12. A ROMANTIC REIGNITION, 1945

There's fun music playing. The good times are back, darling!

Narration.

J: It's a few months after the end of the War and George Buthlay is staying in a reasonably grand hotel near the Palace—

MARION: He is?

J: He's got an interview to work at a new bank in London—

MARION: He has?

J: He's pretty sure he'll get it when he's able to drop an impressive connection or two—

MARION: He's not a bit like that—

J: We're all a bit like that—

They agree to meet in the bar of the reasonably grand hotel near the Palace—

MARION: I've aged.

J: Just put your lippy on and get to the bar.

> *Lippy goes on.* MARION *gets to the bar. She can't help enjoying the music, the vibe, being out! She doesn't see* GEORGE *arrive at first. When they meet, the chemistry is still there, palpably.*
>
> *Dialogue.*

MARION: I thought you were done with London.

GEORGE: I thought I should ascertain, with your Lilibet all grown up, whether you'd be in need of something to do with your time. Someone else to care for.

MARION: The Queen wants me here until Margo is a grown-up.

Then I get a pension, and a place at Kensington Palace.

Mind you—I suspect Margo could live until she's ninety and still be a child—

GEORGE: A pension and a free house at Kensington Palace?

MARION: Kensington Palace copped it during the Blitz.

I'm not sure I want to live in actual rubble.

GEORGE: Free royal rubble.

MARION: I've been doing what the Queen wants for fourteen years.
    What about my life? What I want?
GEORGE: Dame Marion Crawford of Kensington Palace on a full royal
    pension?
    What could be better?
MARION: Being Mrs George Buthlay in a detached house on a hill in
    Aberdeen?
GEORGE: That's very direct.
MARION: Living through two world wars will do that to a woman.
    What's the point of waiting about?

    Beat.

GEORGE: Marion, I don't have anything.
    The war. It cleaned me out.

    Beat.

How much longer with Margaret?
MARION: Two years.
GEORGE: What's another two years?
    In the grand scheme of our romance?
    What's another two years if it earns us a free house and a pension?
MARION: Two years is a long time for a woman my age who's always
    wanted her own children.
GEORGE: It will set us up! A Kensington Palace address for a banker?
    We can sing and dance and have fish suppers by the Thames at
    the weekends.
    We can work and save.
    We can marry when you finish up with Margaret, we can live in
    the house they give you and we can save more!
    We'll have that detached house on the hill in Aberdeen in no
    time.
MARION: You're saying 'yes'?
GEORGE: I've waited on your terms before Marion.
    I think you can wait on mine?
    After everything I've gone through with those wars, fighting for
    empires that shouldn't even exist?
    I'd love to live in one of their palaces for a wee bit.

I've earned it, don't you think?

We've earned it.

Let's drink to it! A double scotch for me and a squash for the lady.

To a wedding, over a decade later!

To a detached house on a hill in Aberdeen!

To two to three wee Marions running wild amongst the purple heather of our very own garden.

13. *AGAIN WITH THE SCUPPERING OF WEDDING PLANS, 1947*

Dialogue.

LILIBET: Crawfie. Might I come in?

MARION: Only if you know the special knock!

> *She knocks a special knock.*

LILIBET: I was with Granny in the vault choosing my wedding jewels and told her all about you and George.

MARION: Queen Mary knows I'm getting married?

LILIBET: We picked the most perfect jewels for you, Crawfie!

> LILIBET *takes off the scarf.* MARION *is stunned, and she hasn't even opened the box.*

Of course they're only a loan.

And they really rather need a more regal bag, don't you think?

MARION: My word.

LILIBET: Crawfie, what's the matter?

MARION: Darling. I didn't think I'd ever have my own wedding—

> *She opens the case. There's a glittering tiara.*

LILIBET: Granny found the matching bracelet for me to wear as your Maid of Honour!

Isn't this heaven?

> LILIBET *puts the tiara on* MARION *and they hug.*

And I've one other tiny present.

You mustn't laugh.

I tried dreadfully hard and you know I'm terrible at knitting—

> *She hands* MARION *some booties.*

For the future Baby Buthlay. Botched booties.

MARION: I love them!

> *Enter* ELIZABETH.

ELIZABETH: Surely you're a both a bit old to be playing dress-ups?

LILIBET: Granny and I picked it out for Crawfie's wedding.

Doesn't she look a dream?

ELIZABETH: Lilibet, I suspect Granny might be getting deficient of a marble or two.

Our jewels don't belong to us—

LILIBET: Yes, we know, Mummy.

But Granny picked these herself for Crawfie—

ELIZABETH: The jewels aren't in Granny's care anymore, Lilibet.

They're in mine.

And they're entrusted to family members only.

LILIBET: Crawfie is family, Mummy.

ELIZABETH: She's not, Lilibet.

I'm sorry, Crawfie, but we'll have to get Ainslie to return them.

MARION: Of course, Ma'am.

It was a lovely thought, Lilibet.

Jewels don't matter though.

The only thing that really matters is that you're there celebrating with me.

ELIZABETH: About that.

> *Beat.*

It's an awfully strange look for you to be married before Lilibet and Philip and … Why on earth would you want Lilibet as your bridesmaid?

MARION: Because—

ELIZABETH: No bride wants to be overshadowed on her special day.

Especially an older bride—

LILIBET: Mummy, I don't like this.

ELIZABETH: Lilibet, there's too much happening here with your own wedding—

LILIBET: We can't possibly miss Crawfie's wedding!

She put off her wedding because of us!

ELIZABETH: And of course we appreciate the many sacrifices dear Crawfie made for us.

We've all made sacrifices, Lilibet.

We've all had to do things we didn't think we'd have to, or want to.

Do you think the last decade has been easy for me?

For your poor father?

LILIBET: No, Mummy.

ELIZABETH: You'll have to get used to making sacrifices.

Your life is going to be making sacrifices—

LILIBET: Mummy—

ELIZABETH: Your royal wedding. The first royal wedding since the War.

You may not be a Hollywood beauty or a dazzling intellect darling, but you need to devote every moment you have— convincing the people you'll be the perfect Queen.

Weddings are how we do that.

But not as a flower girl at the wedding of your former nanny. For goodness' sake.

LILIBET: Mummy.

ELIZABETH: I'm terribly sorry but we won't make it.

Lilibet won't be your bridesmaid.

Of course we'll send a lovely gift and card you can show your family and friends in Scotland.

You mean so much to us, you really do.

LILIBET: But—

ELIZABETH: You're not a girl anymore, Lilibet.

You're about to be a wife.

And one day, hopefully when you're a very old woman, the Queen.

Beat.

ELIZABETH *exits.*

MARION *begins to take off the tiara and return it to the box.*

MARION: A courageous person does the hard thing, Lilibet.

A courageous person acts with integrity.

LILIBET: She's right.

It's right I stay in London and prepare for my wedding.

MARION: I'll miss you at mine.

LILIBET: I will expect a very detailed, minute by minute description.

Of everything.

Will you save me a piece of wedding cake?

MARION: I will.

Narration.

As she walks away, I remember her tiny hand.

How warm and soft it was.

How it used to fit perfectly in mine.

J: At the age of thirty-eight, Marion Kirk Crawford becomes Mrs George Buthlay at the altar of Dunfermline Abbey.

It's a small wedding.

They send a tea set as a token of their happy wishes for the couple's future.

After Lilibet's wedding, Margo comes of age and the Queen finally sets Marion free.

Thirty eight and retires her out.

Like Black Beauty in the final chapter of Lilibet's beloved tale.

What now?

She's never made a dame, but she is given an honour reserved for loyal staff: 'distinguished personal service to the monarch.'

One month into retirement, no pregnancy.

Five months into retirement, no pregnancy.

A year into retirement—you get it.

No children to call Marion 'Mummy' or George 'Papa'.

When Black Beauty retired, he said 'My troubles are all over and I am at home.'

Not so for Marion Crawford.

Our workhorse in her crumbling stable—Nottingham Cottage.

14. MEET BRUCE GOULD, 1949

Bruce Gould is bright and shiny and full of America.

BRUCE: Listen. I know the ladies.

I came from one. I'm married to one. I know what they like to read. When they like to read. And how they like to read it.

And here's what they like to read, the ladies: they like stories that take you behind the scenes of the ladies they like.

And you know what? We're heading into the 1950s and the modern ladies? They like this Princess Elizabeth.

She's homely enough she could be their friend, but she's also a princess. A real-life princess with a war-hero husband who looks like he's straight out of the pictures of a fairytale book. The fairytale book they loved reading as a girl.

So yeah. We need stories about Princess Elizabeth. How she came to be Princess Elizabeth. From someone who knows her. No stuffy, snobby writers on the royal teat.

A friend maybe? Do princesses even have friends? See! These are the things the ladies need to know.

15. EVERYTHING IS FALLING APART, 1950

GEORGE *is having a wee dram or ten.* MARION *trips over some rubble.*
Narration.

MARION: A Kensington Palace address might sound grand.
It's not.
Nottingham Cottage was built in the late 1600s—
And I'm not entirely sure it's had any work done on it since.

> *Dialogue.*

GEORGE: Oh for Christ's sake.
I'm yet to be a day in here without bumping my head on something or finding a chunk of cement in my whiskey.

MARION: It's you who wanted to live here—

GEORGE: Well I don't now. I've had enough—

MARION: I wouldn't mind it if you didn't sit around complaining about it all day—

GEORGE: Is that your way of telling me to get a job, Marion?
No-one wants a worker over fifty.

MARION: No-one wants a worker who arrives hungover each morning, I'd imagine.

GEORGE: You wait here day after day.
For her visits.
She has a life now, Marion.
And extra extra read all about it, Marion.
You're not part of it.

MARION: You're in a rather sour mood today, George.

GEORGE: That English accent you put on with them is embarrassing.
'It was so delightful to see Queen Mary looking so fit and well.'
Seventeen years of your life you gave them.
And they put us in what's no more than a derelict old bedsit, on a pension that makes us prisoners—

MARION: What else can I do?

GEORGE: That there carpet bag?
The only thing in this cottage more haggard than you?

You can pick it up, take the bus down to Sotheby's auction house.

And sell those dirty letters she wrote you about her cousin.

MARION: George!

GEORGE: Or the card from a sixteen-year-old Margaret telling you about what she and that married bastard Townsend got up to in Cape Town—

You may have taught those girls to read, Marion.

MARION: How dare you go through my things!

GEORGE: But you certainly didn't teach them any morals.

MARION: What's in that bag is private!

GEORGE: What's in that bag is worth a fortune.

MARION: It's not for sale.

It will never be for sale.

They're my memories.

My keepsakes.

They trusted me.

GEORGE: Your Lilibet will be the Queen someday.

There's value in all of it.

The ticket stubs.

That wee lock of her hair.

The letters.

Christ. What you could sell the letters for.

All that crap in them. Sell them. Move on.

Let's start afresh away from them all.

The stuff from the bag is all over the floor. MARION *picks it up carefully.*

16. AMERICAN PR, 1949

Dialogue.

BRUCE: Bruce Gould, *Ladies Home Journal*, USA.

What do I call ya honey?

My Queen?

Your Royal Highness?

Mrs George Vee One?

ELIZABETH: Your Majesty will do, Mr Gould.

BRUCE: Seems pretty damn stuffy for a sweet peach like you!

ELIZABETH: Should we like each other, it's a graduation to Queenie-Poo.

BRUCE: I love it.

I know people, Your Maj, and you're good people.

ELIZABETH: 'Your Maj'? Naughty!

BRUCE: Let's get to it, QP.

My magazine.

The women of America love it. In their millions.

And they love your daughter.

I'm told, by my terrifically placed sources in your foreign office, they think it would be just the ticket for us to work together.

ELIZABETH: It took rather a long time for your countrymen to enter the War.

Our diplomats seem to think some American PR might have you leap to our defence a little earlier next time.

BRUCE: They're bang on Queenie-Poo!

Let's do this.

ELIZABETH: Do what?

BRUCE: Your daughter.

Queen in waiting and all that.

What are her hobbies? What did she do during the War? Where did she go to school?

ELIZABETH: She didn't go to school—

BRUCE: What?

See?

I'm interested already!

We do a series of these articles over a few months.

See how the readers respond. See if they want more.

They will, so we do more.

ELIZABETH: Would you be writing these 'articles'?

BRUCE: God no.

I'm the editor.

I make sure they ping-a-ding-ding-ding.

We'd look for a writer. A journalist.

Probably over here.

Someone who gets you lot.

And gets what we want.

ELIZABETH: I have a recommendation for you Gouldy Schmouldy—

How do you like that?

BRUCE: I love it.

ELIZABETH: There's a journalist at *The Times*.

A Mr Dermot Morrah. Terribly nice chap.

Written a few of the King's speeches.

His most recent book was last year's smash hit, *The British Red Cross*.

BRUCE: Sounds riveting.

ELIZABETH: He knows us all.

We trust him.

We could arrange access to Queen Mary, some of Lilibet's cousins, her old nanny, Crawfie—

BRUCE: There's a nanny?

Goddamn.

Can she tell a story?

ELIZABETH: I suppose so.

BRUCE: Where's she nannying now?

ELIZABETH: She's retired and in a cottage at Kensington Palace.

BRUCE: Damn. So she's old?

Is she cute-and-cuddly old at least?

ELIZABETH: She's barely forty.

BRUCE: A young nanny? Retired?

ELIZABETH: She took care of the girls through the abdication, through the War.

She's a remarkable person.

Very loyal.

Of course we'd only have a remarkable person who's very loyal.

BRUCE: Loyal. Got it.

Queenie Royal loves a loyal.

ELIZABETH: She knows Lilibet almost better than any other.

She earned her retirement.

She really did.

BRUCE: When can I meet her?

ELIZABETH: We can put Mr Morrah in touch with her?

BRUCE: It's the nanny who needs to do the articles.

What would you prefer to read?

Some schmuck whose passion in life is the British Red Cross?

Or the soft and gentle recollections of the sweet English nanny?

ELIZABETH: She's Scottish.

BRUCE: Scottish!

Even better!

ELIZABETH: Crawfie does love Lilibet—

BRUCE: 'Crawfie'?

ELIZABETH: Her name before marriage was Marion Crawford.

We call her 'Crawfie'.

BRUCE: You English! What a hoot!

17. A FAUSTIAN DEAL IS DONE, 1950

Dialogue.

MARION: Eighty-five thousand dollars. In pounds, that's—
BRUCE: You've never seen that much cash before, have ya honey?
Mind if I call ya honey?
It'll get you out of this dump—

Narration.

MARION: Money, and Americans, they make me nervous.
George loves him. George loves money.
George looks over the contract. Thinks it's fine.
Thinks finally someone is putting a value on what I hold in my memory.
Of course I'd be lying if I didn't tell you I spend a good amount of time dreaming about what the money could do.
I'm worried about what Lilibet might think.
She's getting ready to have a baby.
She hasn't been by in an age.
And I don't know a world where the Queen would approve of such a thing.

Dialogue.

BRUCE: Would Queenie have introduced us to each other if she didn't think it was the greatest idea in the history of women's publishing?
MARION: But the things I'd be telling you.
They've been private until now.
BRUCE: I think the articles should actually form a book.
How about that?
We run them in the *Ladies Home Journal* in the US, then we turn them into a book.
Called *The Little Princesses*!
Goddamn, they'll fly off the shelves.
The whole world will be in love with them.
Here's what I'll need from you.

Time. A month or so.

You'll be meeting with Dorothy Black.

She's an excellent Scottish ghost writer.

MARION: I'm perfectly capable of writing the stories myself.

BRUCE: Oh no, honey.

People never write their own books.

Ghost writers are essential.

Especially for a top-end story like this.

It's their bread and butter to craft what we call 'a narrative' in the biz.

I'm sure you're a wonderful storyteller, and we need that captured, but believe me honey, you want a ghost writer.

You tell her your terrific stories.

She writes them up.

It's gotta be written right, baby.

You'll approve them.

MARION: If I'm not writing my stories, what are you paying me for?

BRUCE: Your proximity! Your name!

Your reputation! Your connections!

Your 'here's how you raise a princess from the person who raised the princess'.

We're paying for you, doll.

Marion Crawford. Crawfie!

The Queen's Nanny!

MARION: Will they approve them too?

BRUCE: You're hardly going to say something that'll upset them, are ya?

I mean, you're welcome to—

MARION: Of course not.

BRUCE: We'll publish in the new year over three issues, and the book will come out afterwards.

Have you ever seen so much money?

Christ! I've never paid so much money.

You're costing me more than my goddamn house.

Sign here.

MARION: And the Queen will sign off after?

BRUCE: The royal tick! You bet, doll.

If you're smart with this cash you won't ever have to work
again—

MARION: I like working, Mr Gould.

BRUCE: What I'm saying is:

The world's gonna be your oyster.

She signs.

18. THE QUEEN VISITS NOTT COTT, 1950

MARION *is setting up tea, as we see her do in the first and last scenes. Perhaps without the same care. She doesn't love Elizabeth like she loves Lilibet.*

Dialogue.

ELIZABETH: Crawfie! Darling! Look at this place.

It's charming. So charming.

Really, very charming.

MARION: Tea?

ELIZABETH: Have you any gin, Crawfie?

Nerves are quite rattled today.

MARION: I've even got some dubbonet if you'd like me to fix you a wee cocktail?

ELIZABETH: Gorgeous dear, thank you.

No need to mention it to the girls.

And as I heard Mr Coward say recently, 'It's five p.m. somewhere.'

MARION: Cheers to that.

MARION *fixes the drinks.*

ELIZABETH: I thought I'd check how things are going along with these articles.

You met with Mr Gould?

MARION: With your permission.

ELIZABETH: He's paying you, yes?

MARION: Yes. American money.

As the book will be published in America first.

ELIZABETH: The book?

I thought it was two or three articles for the *Ladies Home Journal.*

MARION: It is.

The book will be the published collection of them.

I've signed the contract, Ma'am.

ELIZABETH: A book is a different matter to some articles.

MARION: George hasn't been happy in London.

This American money means we can afford to get back to Scotland, Ma'am.

I couldn't be more grateful to you.

For recommending me for this opportunity.

ELIZABETH: Mr Gould knows, doesn't he, that you absolutely can't have your name on these articles … this book?

We can't have someone who was with our family for years and years revealing what they saw—

MARION: I thought that's what you—what Mr Gould—I thought that was the agreement?

ELIZABETH: Yes, but not a book and not with your name attached.

MARION: I daresay, Ma'am, the money I'm being offered—and it's a lot of money—is precisely because of my name.

To the Americans, I'm of value.

My name.

My years with the family.

ELIZABETH: Might I remind you, serving this family is an honour.

It's an honour only the finest people are selected for.

Those with the utmost discretion—

MARION: Ma'am. They're my stories too—

ELIZABETH: They're 'your' stories too?

Whatever do you mean?

MARION: Lilibet's stories are my stories.

I tucked her in most nights.

I slept, I woke, I lived my life for her. And Margaret.

To deliver them to you for half an hour each day, the perfect little girls you remember.

Mothering them so you could get on with the business of being Queen.

You do realise mothering them means I never mothered my own?

Beat.

ELIZABETH: One would have rather preferred to spend more time than half an hour a day with them, Crawfie, but one didn't have the choice—

MARION: Yes, Ma'am.

And it was the privilege of my life to be there for them.

ELIZABETH: It was your job.

> And you did that job very well.
>
> No-one's saying you didn't.

> *Beat.*

I need to protect us all, dear.

> The girls, of course, from gossip. The King, of course, from himself.
>
> And you, Crawfie.
>
> You enjoy such a fine reputation now. Such fine connections.
>
> We wouldn't want the world to think you're not the discreet, loyal member of the family you are, would we?
>
> That you'd make up stories for a few extra pounds?

> *Beat.*

MARION: You've known me most of my adult life.

> Have I ever once made up a story? Told you a lie?

ELIZABETH: None of us have perfect memories, dear.

MARION: I recorded everything.

> I kept everything.
>
> A diary from my first day at One-Four-Five Piccadilly.
>
> Every letter the girls wrote me.
>
> Every note slipped under my door at night.
>
> Seventeen years of personal messages from you and the King—

ELIZABETH: You did?

> Well that does sound like quite the archive you've amassed.

MARION: I knew I was entrusted somewhere special.

> I didn't want to forget a thing.

> *Beat.*

ELIZABETH: Goodness.

> I'd love to get my hands on that diary some day.
>
> I've never been disciplined enough for a diary.
>
> I expect I'll have to rely on some poor historian putting together my letters for anything resembling one.

> *Beat.*

One more thing—

I think we might need to find a different apartment for you.
This cottage is rather small.
And I don't know if you've noticed, but—
Your posture is somewhat crouched since you've been here.
Most unlike you.

MARION *curtsies.* ELIZABETH *exits.*

19. THE BOOK IS TOLD, 1950

Narration.

MARION: I go each day to the Dorchester Hotel and tell the ghost writer my stories.

Fancy being paid so much money just to sit in a room and tell my stories?

She cares about my stories.

She says they're important stories.

Who gets to see a little girl grow up to be a queen?

I read some of the ghost writer's first chapters.

I suppose it sounds like me.

J: It doesn't sound like you.

MARION: A record of a sweet lady spending time with a sweet family.

J: Hardly a page-turner.

MARION: There's no way the Queen or Lilibet will be aggrieved.

J: You keep telling yourself that.

You sold your story and it's not even in your voice.

MARION: My name on the cover of a book.

Have you ever had your name on the cover of a book?

J: Of course.

Rupert's royal correspondent for decades?

Of course I wrote a book.

I've written book-s.

MARION: What are you talking about?

J: There's a price to every book though, haven't you heard?

Every story.

Every storyteller.

Every book.

If you're doing your job, you're selling someone out.

If you're doing your job properly, you're selling out a whole tribe.

That's what the money's really for.

MARION: Mr Churchill's nanny never got her name on the cover of a book.

What was her name again?

J: Everest.

Churchill's nanny's name was Mrs Elizabeth Anne Everest.

20. THE QUEEN READS THE BOOK, 1950

Dialogue.

AINSLIE: Your Majesty, the 'first edition'.

Hot off the presses, as I believe they say in the book biz.

ELIZABETH: Did you really hand it to me without a drink, Ainslie?

Well, well, well.

The Little Princesses.

By Marion Crawford.

'For seventeen years governess to the Royal Family.'

> AINSLIE *fetches her a drink. She begins to read. Drains her drink.* AINSLIE *gets another. Takes to the book with her pen. Drains the new drink.* AINSLIE *gets another, et cetera.*

Ainslie.

I think the nanny has gone quite off her head.

This will not do.

Was there a privacy clause in your contract of employment?

AINSLIE: No, Ma'am.

ELIZABETH: Well, you can expect to be getting one. You all will.

Even that chap that lays out the rat baits.

Every one of you will be signing a privacy clause.

AINSLIE: [*affronted*] Yes, Ma'am.

ELIZABETH: If the nanny can't be trusted, can anyone be trusted?

Have you made a deal with a publisher, Ainslie?

Got yourself a literary agent?

Planning on selling your royal cocktail recipes to fulfil a lifelong dream to renovate a chateau in the south of France?

AINSLIE: No, Ma'am.

ELIZABETH: You'd think from this book the King is a madman and Lilibet has some sort of compulsive cleaning disorder!

AINSLIE: Yes, Ma'am.

ELIZABETH: And, Ainslie, you have quite the starring role too—

AINSLIE: I do, Ma'am?

Goodness.

ELIZABETH: 'Goodness' is right.

Ainslie.

> *Beat.*

Have the Christmas cards gone out?

AINSLIE: No, Ma'am. Not until Friday.

ELIZABETH: You'll remove Crawfie's, Mrs Buthlay's—'The Queen's Nanny'—whatever she's calling herself now.

Mrs Buthlay is no longer received by the King and Queen.

No need to keep oyster about that should anyone enquire.

> *He exits. She keeps reading. With reaction. With alcohol. With huffs and exclamations at certain lines. All sorts of emotions: outrage, boredom, incredulity, et cetera.*

How do we solve a problem like … Marion Crawford?

> *Enter* BERTIE, *with a copy of the book.*

BERTIE: Seems to me like a rather dramatic spat in the hen house.

I don't know why you're so upset Buffy, the old girl makes us all sound rather normal.

ELIZABETH: We are not normal!

To be normal is death for us, Bertie!

You should read what she wrote about you and your temper—

BERTIE: Might do my reputation well to be thought of as having a temper.

People do think I'm rather soft, Buffy—

ELIZABETH: I'll have Gould take it out—

BERTIE: She was always such a jolly girl, so happy to be part of things.

Knew when to step away and let us be Mummy and Papa.

It's not so ghastly—

ELIZABETH: It is, Bertie!

What if all the staff think they can do this now?

Next, the stable hand will think he can write, and there's a book about the ups and downs of the royal mews!

I don't think so.

BERTIE: I suspect we're quite safe from an exposé on the bowel motions of the royal ponies.

The stable hand can barely put three words together—

ELIZABETH: You're one to talk!

    I'm sorry, Bertie.

    That was cruel.

    See what this is doing to me?

> *She continues to obsessively read, react and scribble in the book as above.*

> *Enter* BRUCE *with a bunch of copies of* The Little Princesses.

ELIZABETH: Mr Gould—this is not—

BRUCE: It's a hit! We have a goddamn hit!

    Queenie-poo, baby doll, you oughta be thrilled!

    Are you thrilled?

    Tell me you're thrilled?

ELIZABETH: I certainly am not thrilled.

BRUCE: You damn well should be!

    This book has sold so many copies—

ELIZABETH: Rather a surprise that it's a book, Mr Gould.

    A book with the nanny's name all over the front cover.

BRUCE: It's so damn loved—

ELIZABETH: Did you not get my list of changes?

BRUCE: Changed everything you asked for that wasn't on the public record, didn't I?

    I had a personal phone call from the President of the USA himself.

ELIZABETH: You did?

BRUCE: He said to me 'Brucey baby, my Bess and Margaret'—his wife and daughter—'My Bess and Margaret can't be in the same room together.

    'Fight over everything.

    'Today I walk into the East Wing and you know what they're doing? Sitting and talking about Lilibet and goddamn Crawfie.'

    Lilibet and Crawfie bringing mothers and daughters together.

    And the Americans and the Britons.

    It's done exactly what you planned.

    Diplomacy, baby!

    You uptight, tea-drinking, colonising bastards will never fight a war without the U S of A again!

ELIZABETH: One feels like one is rather exposed.

BRUCE: Exposed?

Exposed as a genius!

It was a genius move the genius day you got in touch with me.

Who'd have thought?

ELIZABETH: We sound rather normal.

BRUCE: Normal?

Listen. I live in the real world, Queenie.

And the real world? They love you and your enchanting family.

Because they love this book.

Now.

You know we need to celebrate.

We live to celebrate, we book people! Dubonnet?

Beat.

ELIZABETH: You must bring Mrs Gould to the palace.

We'll have a special garden party for you.

BRUCE: With those coffee sugar lumps from elevenses?

In the book?

ELIZABETH: The King might even demonstrate his excellent hopscotch skills.

Of course it will be a private celebration, Gouldy.

You'll need to keep oyster?

He snaps an oyster with his hands and winks.

Oh, and that ghost writer.

The romance novelist?

Shouldn't we thank her?

Might she like to be celebrated at a garden party?

I've never had a bestseller before!

I suppose it does feel rather lovely!

21. A BESTSELLING AUTHOR SLASH PARIAH 1950–1988

Narration.

J: Yeah, you heard right.

No garden party invite for Marion.

MARION: I wouldn't have been able to go anyway.

I'm moving back to Scotland and being a bestselling author.

J: Can the Great Royal Traitor enjoy being a bestselling author?

MARION: I have invitations to speak all over Britain.

All over the world!

J: You go overseas to tell your stories?

MARION: There's enough happening here as the first 'royal commentator'—

J: How does that work? A royal commentator without any access to the royals?

MARION: Try finding anyone who knows them as well as me.

J: And is willing to talk about them (for a fee)!

MARION: I write five more books!

J: Your ghost writer writes five more books.

MARION: I have a column in *Woman's Own*.

Do you know how many women read *Woman's Own*?

J: Tell them what happens there.

MARION: Such a silly mix-up.

J: Your column is published—it describes your time watching a lush royal ceremony in London.

Only the ceremony never happened, and you're clearly in Aberdeen.

It exposes you as being full of it—

MARION: It exposes my ghost writer as being research-deficient.

J: And it ends you as royal commentator.

You're a tabloid joke. The Brits, they love a tabloid joke.

Then they forget you. Move on to the next tabloid joke.

MARION: Would the stories of a tabloid joke be in every single biography written about Lilibet, the Queen Mother or Margaret?

Everything anyone knows about Lilibet's childhood comes from my book.

Can a tabloid joke be the 'most quoted royal historian' of the twentieth century?

J: Must have been lonely when the stories run out.

And the requests stop coming.

And it's only the 1950s.

You've got decades to live as the one frozen out.

MARION: It's wonderful. To have time to devote to George.

J: Decades to devote to George? Hope he's curbed his dram consumption?

MARION: It takes time to make a marriage work.

To make a home beautiful.

Our detached house on a hill in Aberdeen.

J: Do you ever hear from her?

Does she ever reply to one of your letters?

The things you knit for her children and then her grandchildren?

Does she ever see you at the window, watching as she drives to Balmoral?

MARION: I have a full and wonderful life.

J: Really? That's not what I heard …

22. LILIBET ATTEMPTS TO BE HUMAN, BALMORAL, 1987

ELIZABETH *is rugged-up and fly fishing soon the River Dee. Every now and then she takes a sip from her flask.* LILIBET *joins her to fish.*

Dialogue.

LILIBET: Mummy, there was post today from Ainslie.
　　　　He had some rather upsetting news.
　　　　About Crawfie.

　　　　　Beat.

　Mummy. I'd like to go and see her.
ELIZABETH: Do what you like.
LILIBET: Ainslie says Mr Buthlay has died and she's all alone.
　　　　He says she took too many pills. She tried to take her own life.
　　　　He says she left a note.

　　　　　LILIBET *hands* AINSLIE*'s letter to her mother, who reads it.*

ELIZABETH: Oh really. How very dramatic.
LILIBET: It's about us, Mummy.
ELIZABETH: It could be about anyone.
LILIBET: 'I can't bear those I love to pass me by on the road'?
　　　　Who else would that be?
　　　　Whenever we drive past that little white cottage I feel I should stop in—

　　　　　Beat.

　I'm going to see her.
ELIZABETH: I don't know why you're telling me if you don't want to be stopped.
　　　　You're quite literally the Queen.
LILIBET: She was quite everything to me as a child—
ELIZABETH: I don't know why you still care—
LILIBET: I don't know why you don't.

　　　　　Beat.

A book from a nanny with harmless stories about children was hardly going to dismantle an entire monarchical system—

ELIZABETH: I didn't know that!

> You haven't seen what I've seen!
>
> You don't know how quickly things can change for people like us, and you don't know what it is that will tip it all over.
>
> I asked her not to do it with her name.
>
> Money was more important to her than you, Lilibet.

LILIBET: I'd like to spend the afternoon with her. What harm is an afternoon?

ELIZABETH: A book is not an article in a newspaper, read, then used to light kindling that afternoon.

> It lasts. It sits in libraries. It becomes the truth.
>
> And look at what she unleashed.
>
> Writers, photographers.
>
> Newspapers, magazines.
>
> They think they have a right to our stories now.
>
> She let them in and now they want it all.
>
> 'How does the Queen take her tea?'
>
> 'How does Diana stay so slim?'
>
> 'Why does Charles talk to his plants?'
>
> While I draw breath I can't forgive her.

> *Beat.*

These salmon are being awfully quiet today.

> *Narration.*

J: Lilibet doesn't go to see her old nanny that afternoon.

> She doesn't go that week, or the week after, or the week after that.
>
> When she's on her way back to London, she thinks she might rather take the train than the car to Aberdeen. The railway line goes nowhere near the white detached house on the North Deeside Road.
>
> As the royal train chugs away from Scotland, thoughts of Crawfie evaporate as she thinks about the work she has ahead— the opening of a flower show, the reading of the red boxes. The marriage problems of three of her children.
>
> By the time she's back at the Palace, Crawfie is gone again, consigned to the recesses of her mind.

23. THE END OF CRAWFIE, 1988

Narration.

J: As she gets older and more infirm, the NHS nurse who visits Marion Crawford three times a week suggests she move her bed to the living room.

Hour by hour now, every hour as it happens, she can look out her window.

MARION: All I can do now is wait by my window.

If she's ever seen one of my letters she'll know—

I'm here by the window.

The years don't matter.

What matters is holding her hand in mine.

J: When she dies in her sleep in the February of 1988, she doesn't know she'll be remembered by every newspaper in the country as the great influencer of Q. E. Two's early life.

And the one ousted.

The first to dish the dirt.

The nanny who hadn't kept oyster.

Lilibet hears the news from her mother over breakfast at Windsor Castle.

They're planning a day out shooting, scanning the papers for favourable mentions when—

ELIZABETH: Oh. It would seem your Crawfie has died, Lilibet.

J: Lilibet says she's sorry to hear it.

Lilibet leaves the table.

Goes to the chapel.

The grief takes her in a way she hadn't expected.

The Queen Mother is informed the Queen won't be shooting that day.

Beat.

Marion Kirk Crawford Buthlay's funeral in Aberdeen is a modest one.

Thirty or so acquaintances.

MARION: What about Lilibet?

Is Lilibet there?

Beat.

J: She doesn't even send a wreath.

Beat.

MARION: That can't be.

J: You don't think I checked?

I tracked down every person who'd been there.

I rang every florist in Aberdeen.

It's my job.

MARION: You're lying.

J: For you, I wish I was.

For me?

Much better story.

MARION: You don't care about my story.

J: All I care about is your story.

MARION: You've spent all night making them feel sorry for me.

Being selective about the facts of my life.

What gives you the right to think you can tell my story any better than any of the others?

J: You think I wanted to be stuck here on the royal rota?

I wanted to be covering the fall of the wall. Brexit. The way the rich have taken everything from the poor in this place.

I wanted to file those stories back to Australia and remind people that it's time we stand on our own feet.

That we don't need to be bound to a family who think it's alright to leave palaces empty, take hundreds of millions of pounds from tax-payers—while their 'subjects' line up at foodbanks and are sleeping on the streets?

But he needed me to report on them like they mattered.

And I'm good at my job, so of course I got sucked in.

You can't see a ninety-year-old put on a bright dress and make small talk with thousands of people over thousands of days and not get sucked in.

I was fascinated with Her when she died.

I wanted to know where she really came from.

No-one before her or from her had any of her commitment and integrity.

I found out about you. That it all came from you.

And I found out how they treated you.

And I found out you're what matters.

You're the story I needed to take back home.

You should be front and centre.

What they did to you.

How they made you part of their story but didn't think your story was important.

It is.

And I'm writing your story.

It'll be in something that's all about you—a play or a movie or a book?

Your stories.

And I'll name it after you and together we'll decide where the flags are planted and see how they like it when someone else decides their story for them and they have no choice in it—

MARION: You say they silenced me?

They didn't think my story was important?

What are you doing here then?

J: I'm telling the story.

I've been telling the story the whole time.

Haven't you been listening to me?

This story.

It ends with that bag.

MARION: Her private letters. Her dreams. Her memories.

J: Worth a fortune.

For decades, every scumbag newspaper hack like me tried to buy it from you.

Royal scholars with fat bank accounts begged you to part with it.

'Look at what she did to you! Give us the loot!'

MARION: Never.

J: And you never did.

MARION: I left it to Lilibet.

J: You left it to Lilibet.

MARION: Of course I did.

> I wanted her to have it. What's in here, it's hers.
> I could sell my stories.
> Hers? They weren't mine to sell.

J: It sits today in the Royal Archive.

> No journalist, no biographer, no playwright—
> None of us can get near it.

> *Beat.*

You're a better person than me.

> I wouldn't see it like that.
> If her words and stories were kindling, I'd have burned them down ten times over for what they did to you—
> What she did to you.

MARION: I need to be by my window.

> I told her I'd be there.
> I need to end the story.
> Please.
> It's my story.
> Let's go back to the beginning.

J: Alright then.

> *We're back at the first scene.* MARION *is preparing to welcome someone to tea, et cetera.*

Waiting for a tea party that will never happen—

> Marion Kirk Crawford watches and watches and watches from her window.

MARION: Of course I watch from my window.

> This window is in prime position.
> Anyone who drives between Aberdeen and Balmoral?
> They have to pass by my window.
> So why wouldn't I watch from my window?
> It's my window at the front of my house.
> I bought it with my money.
> I'll watch whomever I want, whenever I want, from whatever damn window I please—

J: Here they come.

What she's waiting for.

The cars.

Newly polished, especially for this trip.

MARION: Police escort out the front.

J: Police escort out the back.

Of course, we all know who's driving the old Land Rover in the middle.

MARION: It's Her.

MARION: Of course it's Her.

J: The cars—

MARION: They make a right—say they make a right!

J: They're making a right.

MARION: They drive up to my gate.

The Land Rover.

It's driving in!

She gets out of the car—say she gets out of the car!

J: She gets out of the car—

MARION: I hear the crunch crunch crunch of her shoes on the pebbles.

There's a knock at the door.

She says, 'Crawfie, might I come in?'

She says, 'Crawfie, might I come in?'

She says—

J: 'Crawfie, might I come in?'

MARION: Only if you know the special knock!

There's a knock of the special knock.

The door opens, MARION *curtsies. She's overjoyed.*

Her tiny hand.

It's warm and soft.

It fits perfectly in mine.

And that's how my story ends. Have you got it?

That's how my story ends.

THE END

THE QUEEN'S NANNY

BY MELANIE TAIT

DIRECTED BY PRISCILLA JACKMAN
ENSEMBLE THEATRE
6 SEPTEMBER 2024 – 12 OCTOBER 2024
WORLD PREMIERE

Ensemble Theatre proudly acknowledges the Cammeraigal people of the Eora nation as customary owners of the land on which we work and share our stories. We pay our respects to Elders past and present.

CAST

MATTHEW BACKER J, NANNY, BERTIE, AINSLIE, LILIBET, GEORGE, BRUCE GOULD

ELIZABETH BLACKMORE MARION

EMMA PALMER ELIZABETH

CREATIVES

PLAYWRIGHT MELANIE TAIT

DIRECTOR PRISCILLA JACKMAN

ASSISTANT DIRECTOR MIRANDA MIDDLETON

SET DESIGNER MICHAEL HANKIN

COSTUME DESIGNER GENEVIEVE GRAHAM

LIGHTING DESIGNER MORGAN MORONEY

COMPOSER & SOUND DESIGNER JAMES PETER BROWN

DIALECT & VOICE COACH JENNIFER WHITE

MOVEMENT COACH TIM DASHWOOD

STAGE MANAGER SEAN PROUDE

ASSISTANT STAGE MANAGER MADELAINE OSBORN

COSTUME SUPERVISOR LILY MATELJAN

RUNNING TIME 90 MINUTES NO INTERVAL

REC. AGES 12+

ADULT THEMES

This production was made possible by Ensemble Theatre's Commissioners' Circle.

The publication of this script was made possible by the generous support of Jenny Reynolds and Guy Reynolds AO.

Special thanks to Currency Press and Melanie Tait.

ABOUT ENSEMBLE THEATRE

Ensemble Theatre is the longest continuously running professional theatre company in Australia and is committed to collaborating with exceptional playwrights and creative talent to present the best international plays, modern classics and new Australian works.

PLAYWRIGHT'S NOTE

I started working on this play around the time the Albanese Labor Government was voted in.

Full of hope, I felt certain when the play got to the stage, we'd have lived through a successful Australian Indigenous Voice Referendum and, in an election year, movement would be ramping up about a new Republic Referendum. I wanted this play to be part of that conversation.

Instead, I write this note a week after a cabinet reshuffle, where, in the wake of last year's referendum, the Albanese Government has abolished the Assistant Ministry for the Republic. We're about to welcome (and spend tax-payer money on) a visit from King Charles III and Queen Camilla, who've just had £45M of public money added to their annual income while the rest of the UK suffers a crippling cost of living crisis.

An Australian Republic is much further away than it was two years ago.

While our Head of State is a man sovereign by accident of birth, in a country on the other side of the earth, THE QUEEN'S NANNY is our story too. I hope it asks questions about the people our society values, and puts Marion Crawford's story front and centre—a working class Scottish woman, shamed and ousted from the family she spent two decades of her life dedicated to.

She was a pioneer: the OG Royal memoirist. Her book was the first insight into the Royals behind closed doors—showing them as a relatively loving, normal family. The Queen Mother's concern about the book was warranted—what would it mean for the people of the British Empire to know they were being 'ruled over' and funding a family who are really a rather average lot?

At the time, it was a PR coup for everyone but Crawfie. In the context of 2024, in a post *Diana: Her True Story* and *Spare* world, Marion Crawford's story adds to the myriad of reasons why the Crown should be relegated to history books and Netflix series, and Australia should stand completely on its own feet.

MELANIE TAIT
PLAYWRIGHT

DIRECTOR'S NOTE

When Melanie first told me about Crawfie's story—a woman who lived in the same town as her own Scottish family, who mixed and worked amongst Melanie's own extended family and friends, after being ousted by the royals—I was surprised it was the first I'd heard of Marion Crawford. In a contemporary world, which seems obsessed with mining all details of royal life for artistic and celebrity click bait, I was shocked Crawfie's story was not more widely known.

However, in reading the first draft of Melanie's beautiful lyrical text, I was instantly moved by the bold form she explores—resisting any depiction of 'The Crown-esque' characterisation—to create a taut, playful, yet deeply affecting commentary on power, authorship, motherhood and loyalty.

THE QUEEN'S NANNY is a play that speaks directly to our Australian audiences, interrogating, through the fallen figure of Crawfie, wider questions around our position culturally and politically within the British Commonwealth. Through Crawfie, we are invited into conversations about who is entitled to tell whose story, and how stories handed down through history are shaped by the powerful. Melanie invites us to reflect on the voiceless women who have raised some of the world's finest leaders and shines a spotlight on the complexities of the roles of the 'surrogate mother' and the loyal subject.

With all of Melanie's characteristic charm, the playful humour and deft dialogue of THE QUEEN'S NANNY and its unequivocal celebration of theatricality, invites us to enjoy a delightful night at the theatre, while raising some rueful provocations around choice, autonomy and the manipulation of the stories we tell ourselves through our shared history.

PRISCILLA JACKMAN
DIRECTOR

MELANIE TAIT
PLAYWRIGHT

Ensemble Theatre: A BROADCAST COUP, THE
APPLETON LADIES' POTATO RACE. Court Theatre,
NZ: THE APPLETON LADIES' POTATO RACE.
Queensland Theatre: THE APPLETON LADIES'
POTATO RACE. State Theatre Company of South
Australia: THE APPLETON LADIES' POTATO RACE.
Old Red Lion Theatre, UK: THE VEGEMITE TALES.
Riverside Studios: THE VEGEMITE TALES. The
Venue (The Leicester Square Theatre), West End,
UK: THE VEGEMITE TALES . Film: THE APPLETON
LADIES' POTATO RACE premiered on Paramount+
and Channel 10. Current commissions: Ensemble
Theatre, Melbourne Theatre Company, Sydney
Festival, National Institute of Dramatic Art and
developing an original tv series with Screen
Tasmania and Screen Australia. Publications: THE
APPLETON LADIES' POTATO RACE, THE QUEEN'S
NANNY published by Currency Press, A
BROADCAST COUP published by Playlab.

PRISCILLA JACKMAN
DIRECTOR

Ensemble Theatre: THE QUEEN'S NANNY, THE
APPLETON LADIES' POTATO RACE, RELATIVELY
SPEAKING, THE IMPORTANCE OF BEING
EARNEST. National Institute of Dramatic Arts: THE
GLASS MENAGERIE, BEYOND THE SKY AND SEA,
EURYDIKE + ORPHEUS, GHOSTS, LOVE AND
HONOUR. National Theatre of Parramatta: GIRLS
IN BOYS CARS. Sydney Theatre Company: RBG:
OF MANY, ONE, WHITE PEARL, STILL POINT
TURNING: THE CATHERINE MCGREGOR STORY.
Western Australian Academy of Performing Arts:
AN IDEAL HUSBAND. Assistant Director: Ensemble
Theatre: GOOD PEOPLE, BAREFOOT IN THE

PARK. Opera Australia: ERNANI, BLUEBEARD'S CASTLE. Sydney Theatre Company: THE HANGING, THE FATHER. Revival Director: Opera Australia: THE BARBER OF SEVILLE, THE MAGIC FLUTE. Co-Director: Sport For Jove: ROMEO AND JULIET, THE TEMPEST.

MIRANDA MIDDLETON
ASSISTANT DIRECTOR

Ensemble Theatre: MASTER CLASS, A LETTER FOR MOLLY. Bell Shakespeare: THE LOVERS, TIMON OF ATHENS, ARDEN OF FAVERSHAM. Dirty Pennies Theatre Project: LEMON TREE ON DREG STREET. JRP Productions: LITTLE WOMEN. Melbourne Theatre Company: COME RAIN OR COME SHINE. Old Fitz Theatre: THE EISTEDDFOD. Rogue Projects: NOT TODAY, PEAR-SHAPED. Salty Theatre: THE GRINNING MAN, VOLDEMORT AND THE TEENAGE HOGWARTS MUSICAL PARODY. Theatre Works: SENSER. Training: National Institute of Dramatic Art.

MATTHEW BACKER
J, NANNY, BERTIE, AINSLIE, LILIBET, GEORGE, BRUCE GOULD

Ensemble Theatre: THE QUEEN'S NANNY. Bell Shakespeare: HENRY V, THE TEMPEST. Belvoir Street Theatre: KILL THE MESSENGER. Dodger Theatricals/New Theatricals: JERSEY BOYS. Griffin Theatre Company: LADIES DAY, THE FOX, THE TORTOISE, WHERE IT ALL BEGAN, UNCANNY VALLEY. Hayes Theatre Company: YOUNG FRANKENSTEIN, ONLY HEAVEN KNOWS. HotHouse Theatre: FRENZY FOR TWO. Queensland Theatre: NEARER THE GODS, SWITZERLAND, BRISBANE. Sydney Opera House/

Peach Theatre Company: THE HISTORY BOYS. Sydney Theatre Company: ON THE BEACH, STRANGE CASE OF DR JEKYLL AND MR HYDE, CLOUD NINE, CHIMERICA, A MIDSUMMER'S NIGHT DREAM, ORLANDO, MACHINAL. Theatre Works St Kilda: PRIVATE VIEW. Film: PLAY DIRTY, THIS TIME MAYBE, MARLEY SOMEONE. Television: PLAY SCHOOL, NEIGHBOURS, PROSPER, FIVE BEDROOMS, WELLMANIA, THE TWELVE, MIKKI VS THE WORLD, JOE VS CAROLE, HARROW, OPERATION BUFFALO, HOME AND AWAY, DEAD LUCKY, HISTORY HUNTERS. Awards: Broadway World Award for Best Actor in a Supporting Role (A MIDSUMMER'S NIGHT DREAM), 2016. Matilda Award for Best Actor in a Play (SWITZERLAND), 2017. Sydney Theatre Award for Best Male Actor in a Supporting Role in a Musical (ONLY HEAVEN KNOWS), 2018. Dendy Award for Best Live Action Australian Short for DIE BULLY DIE (Screenwriter, Producer and Actor), 2024.

ELIZABETH BLACKMORE
MARION

GWB: DEATH OF A SALESMAN (Sydney and Melbourne Seasons). Black Swan State Theatre Company: THE VIBRATOR PLAY, A MIDSUMMER NIGHT'S DREAM, MUCH ADO ABOUT NOTHING. Barking Gecko: JASPER JONES. Belvoir Street Theatre: A MIDSUMMER NIGHT'S DREAM. Film: SKIN DEEP, THE BURNING MAN, EVIL DEAD, SLEEPING DOGS. Television: THE RIGHT STUFF, SHAMELESS, SHOOTER, AUGUST CREEK, ONCE UPON A TIME, BEAUTY AND THE BEAST, TURN: WASHINGTON'S SPIES, LEGEND OF THE SEEKER, HOME AND AWAY, SUPERNATURAL, THE VAMPIRE DIARIES. Training: Western Australian Academy of Performing Arts.

EMMA PALMER
ELIZABETH

Ensemble Theatre: BENEFACTORS, CRUNCH TIME, RELATIVELY SPEAKING. Critical Stages: SYNCOPATION. Darlinghurst Theatre: KINDERTRANSPORT, REMEMBERING PIRATES, CONSTELLATIONS, RIDE, FOURPLAY, THE JUNGLE. Griffin Theatre: THE KID, ON THE SHORE OF THE WIDE WORLD. Melbourne Festival: THE TROUBLE WITH HARRY. Sport for Jove: ROMEO & JULIET, WAR OF THE ROSES. Sydney Theatre Company: TOT MOM, THE LOST ECHO. The National Theatre UK/Global Creatures: WAR HORSE. Television: PLAYSCHOOL, PIECES OF HER, ALL SAINTS, UNDERBELLY: A TALE OF TWO CITIES, OFFSIDE, BIKIE WARS, GASP! Training: National Institute of Dramatic Art.

MICHAEL HANKIN
SET DESIGNER

Ensemble Theatre: WHO'S AFRAID OF VIRGINIA WOOLF, LIBERTY EQUALITY FRATERNITY and GREAT FALLS. Opera Australia: IL TRITTICO. STC: ON THE BEACH, JUMPY. Belvoir Street Theatre: INTO THE WOODS, THE BOOMKAK PANTO, WAYSIDE BRIDE, LIGHT SHINING IN BUCKINGHAMSHIRE, THE GLASS MENAGERIE, HIR, ANGELS IN AMERICA, GHOSTS, IVANOV, TWELFTH NIGHT, THE SUGARHOUSE, THE GREAT FIRE, MARK COLVIN'S KIDNEY and THE DARKROOM. Griffin Theatre: GOLDEN BLOOD, UGLY MUGS. Bell Shakespeare: THE MERCHANT OF VENICE, AS YOU LIKE IT and OTHELLO. Barbican Centre: MEMORIAL. Manchester's Home Theatre: INSANE ANIMALS. Brink Productions: THE ASPIRATIONS OF DAISE MORROW and TARTUFFE. Theatre Royal: DIRTY ROTTEN

SCOUNDRELS. Chunky Move/Malthouse Theatre: 247 DAYS. Force Majeure: YOU ANIMAL YOU and FLOCK. Film: Michael was the art director for Ireland's 2020 entry for EUROVISION, the challenge designer for SURVIVOR AUSTRALIA (S6) and the weapons designer/co-ordinator for THREE THOUSAND YEARS OF LONGING. Training: National Institute of Dramatic Art.

GENEVIEVE GRAHAM
COSTUME DESIGNER

Ensemble Theatre: DIPLOMACY, THE APPLETON LADIES' POTATO RACE, THE LAST FIVE YEARS, MURDER ON THE WIRELESS, A CHRISTMAS CAROL, BOXING DAY BBQ. The Brandenburg Orchestra: HANDEL'S MESSIAH, BITTERSWEET OBSESSIONS, NOTRE DAME. The Theatre of Image: BRETT AND WENDY: A LOVE STORY BOUND BY ART. Television: Costume designer; APPETITE (SBS), THE DISPOSABLES (ABC), OPTICS (ABC COMEDY). Costume assistant; THE COMMONS (STAN). Costume buyer; HEARTBREAK HIGH SEASONS 1&2, PAPERDOLLS, COLIN FROM ACCOUNTS SEASON 2. Short film: Costume Designer; DOG EATS WORLD, LUNA AND THE BRAIN TUNA. Feature Film: Costume assistant; SHANG-CHI, THOR: LOVE AND THUNDER. Training: National Institute of Dramatic Art. Awards: 2017 Emerging Designer for Live Performance for EURYDIKE AND ORPHEUS (A NIDA production).

MORGAN MORONEY
LIGHTING DESIGNER

Ensemble Theatre: THE QUEEN'S NANNY, SUDDENLY LAST SUMMER, CLYDE'S, MR BAILEY'S MINDER. Australian Brandenburg Orchestra: INFERNO. Australian Theatre for Young People: SAPLINGS, SHACK. Belvoir Street Theatre: NAYIKA: A DANCING GIRL, SHITTY. Essential Workers: COLLAPSIBLE. National Theatre of Parramatta: GIRLS IN BOYS CARS, A PRACTICAL GUIDE TO SELF-DEFENCE. Opera Australia: BARBER OF SEVILLE. Pinchgut Opera: DIDO AND AENEAS. Redline Productions: CLEANSED. Siren Theatre & WorldPride: CAMP. Sugary Rum Productions: ANATOMY OF A SUICIDE. Video Designer: Ensemble Theatre: UNQUALIFIED, A LETTER FOR MOLLY. National Theatre of Parramatta: A PRACTICAL GUIDE TO SELF-DEFENCE. Assistant Lighting Designer: Opera Australia: PHANTOM OF THE OPERA. Associate Lighting Designer: Sport for Jove: OTHELLO. Sydney Theatre Company: DRACULA.

JAMES PETER BROWN
COMPOSER AND SOUND DESIGNER

Belvoir Street Theatre: ICH NIBBER DIBBER, OEDIPUS SCHMOEDIPUS, WHO'S THE BEST? Carriageworks: LAKE DISAPPOINTMENT. CDP: THE MIDNIGHT GANG. Darlinghurst Theatre: LET THE RIGHT ONE IN, IN REAL LIFE, BROKEN ERTH: ARC, SHARK DIVE, WINTER CAMP, THE LIMINAL HOUR, BIRDFOXMONSTER. Griffin Theatre Company: WHEREVER SHE WANDERS, SMURF IN WANDERLAND, TRIBUNAL. Malthouse Theatre: REVOLT. SHE. SAID. REVOLT AGAIN. Sydney Theatre Company: STOLEN, CONSTELLATIONS, DO NOT GO GENTLE…, HOME, I'M DARLING,

RULES FOR LIVING, THE DEEP BLUE SEA, THE REAL THING, LORD OF THE FLIES, MOSQUITOES. Sport for Jove: ROSE RIOT. Windmill Theatre: SUNRUNNERS. SOIT (Belgium): NOMADS, WE WAS THEM, MESSIAH RUN, THE LEE ELLROY SHOW. Film: BIRTHRIGHT, COSMOGRAPHIES, BLOODLINKS, WE CIRCLE SILENTLY, FUNGUS, VOICE ACTIVATED, A BRILLIANT GENOCIDE, BROWN LIPS. TV: TOP OF THE LAKE SEASON 1, THE MOVEMENT. Games: FALLOUT 4, FALLOUT 76, FALLOUT SHELTER. Dance: Raghav Handa: THE ASSEMBLY, FOLLIES OF GOD, CULT OF THE TITANS. Queensland Ballet: TETHERED. Kristina Chan: A FAINT EXISTENCE, BRIGHTNESS, MOUNTAIN. Victoria Hunt: COPPER PROMISES, TANGI WAI. The Australian Ballet: SCOPE. Sydney Dance Company: CONFORM. Matthew Day: THOUSANDS, CANNIBAL, INTERMISSION.

JENNIFER WHITE
DIALECT AND VOICE COACH

Ensemble Theatre: over 18 plays including DEATH OF A SALESMAN, TUESDAYS WITH MORRIE, RAIN MAN, LADIES IN LAVENDER, THE LITTLE DOG LAUGHED, MY WONDERFUL DAY, BROOKLYN BOY. Belvoir Street Theatre: THE DROVER'S WIFE, MORTIDO, THE WOLVES, MY BRILLIANT CAREER. Melbourne Theatre Company: JULIA, SOLOMON AND MARIAN. Opera Australia: WEST SIDE STORY. Sydney Opera House: IN THE HEIGHTS, MIRACLE CITY. Sydney Theatre Company: 11 plays including RBG: OF MANY, ONE, JULIA, ON THE BEACH, A RAISIN IN THE SUN. Film: I AM WOMAN, PETER RABBIT, MORTAL KOMBAT, CARMEN, SERIOUSLY RED, JASPER JONES, TOP END WEDDING, THE HUNTER, CARGO. Television: BALI 2002, PIECES OF HER, STATELESS, A PLACE TO CALL HOME, BIKIE WARS, PACKED TO THE RAFTERS. Training: National Institute of Dramatic Art, ISCD, Theatre Nepean.

TIM DASHWOOD
MOVEMENT COACH

Theatre: Ensemble Theatre: ULSTER AMERICAN, ALONE IT STANDS. Australian Theatre for Young People: SAPLINGS, THE DEB, INTERSECTIONS: ARRIVAL, WAR CRIMES. Bell Shakespeare: THE PLAYERS. Belvoir: TELL ME I'M HERE, FANGIRLS, OPENING NIGHT, THE LIFE OF GALILEO. Darlinghurst Theatre Company: LET THE RIGHT ONE IN. Griffin Theatre Company: JAILBABY, THE LEWIS TRILOGY. Hayes Theatre Company: ZOMBIE! THE MUSICAL, GENTLEMEN PREFER BLONDES, DUBBO CHAMPIONSHIP WRESTLING. National Theatre of Parramatta: GIRLS IN BOYS' CARS. Opera Australia: WEST SIDE STORY, MISS SAIGON, WHITELEY, KROL ROGER, FAUST. shake & stir theatre co.: FOURTEEN, FANTASTIC MR FOX, JANE EYRE. Sydney Theatre Company: A FOOL IN LOVE, THE IMPORTANCE OF BEING EARNEST, JULIUS CAESAR, DEATH OF A SALESMAN, NO PAY? NO WAY!, LORD OF THE FLIES. Other: President of the Society of Australian Fight Directors incorporated.

SEAN PROUDE
STAGE MANAGER

THE QUEEN'S NANNY marks Sean's debut with Ensemble Theatre. Theatre: Bell Shakespeare: MUCH ADO ABOUT NOTHING, JULIUS CAESAR. Belvoir Street Theatre: MORTIDO. Opera Australia: MY FAIR LADY, TURANDOT, AIDA, THE MAGIC FLUTE, MADAMA BUTTERFLY. State Theatre Company of South Australia: LADY DAY AT EMERSONS BAR AND GRILL. Sydney Festival: SEND FOR NELLIE. Sydney Theatre Company: AMERICAN SIGNS, NO PAY NO WAY, THE GOAT AND WHO IS SYLVIA, THE TEMPEST, THE TENANT OF WILDFELL HALL, TRIPLE X, HOW TO RULE THE WORLD, STILL POINT TURNING. Television: BIG BROTHER SERIES 3, ATP CUP TENNIS AUSTRALIA. Training: Western Australian Academy of Performing Arts.

MADELAINE OSBORN
ASSISTANT STAGE MANAGER

Stage Manager: Arts on Tour and Lingua Franca: HIGHWAY OF LOST HEARTS. Branch Nebula: AIR TIME. Force Majeure for Biennale of Sydney: POWER. Griffin Theatre Company: JAILBABY, GHOSTING THE PARTY, IS THERE SOMETHING WRONG WITH THAT LADY? Performing Lines: SUNSHINE SUPER GIRL. Development Workshop supported by Australia Council for the Arts: GRLZ. Assistant Stage Manager: Belvoir Street Theatre: MASTER & MARGARITA. Pinchgut Opera: GIUSTINO, MEDÉE, THE LOVES OF DAPHNE AND APOLLO. Directors incorporated.

LILY MATELJAN
COSTUME SUPERVISOR

Costume Designer/Supervisor: Belvoir Street Theatre: PROPOISE POOL 25A SEASON. Hayes Theatre Co: LITTLE WOMEN. Kings Cross Theatre on Broadway (KXT): RHOMBIOD, GRAIN IN THE BLOOD. Costume Supervisor: Australian Brandenburg Orchestra: INFERNO. Pinchgut Opera: DIDO AND AENEAS. National Institute of Dramatic Arts Production Seasons: A VERY EXPENSIVE POISON (Paid Professional), ALL THAT GLITTERS IS NOT MOULD, FALSETTOS, BETH. Head of Wardrobe: Victorian Opera: IL TABARRO. Films: APPLETON LADIES POTATO RACE, FIVE BLIND DATES. TV: HOUSE OF GODS, THE TWELVE (Season 1), HARDBALL (Season 2), THE OTHER GUY (Season 2). Training: National Institute of Dramatic Art, (BFA Costume) ENMORE DESIGN CENTRE. Awards: Nominated Best Costume Design for RHOMBOID at Sydney Broadway Awards 2023.

SUPPORT US

Every dollar counts. Ensemble relies on self-earned income to deliver all the programs that we do – commissioning new work, education outreach, producing world premieres, so please think about your capacity to make a gift to Ensemble. You can donate online at ensemble.com.au/support-us or contact Stephen Attfield, Philanthropy & Partnerships Manager, on **stephena@ensemble.com.au** or via **02 8918 3400**.

LIFE PATRONS

Those who have made significant contributions to Ensemble:
The Balnaves Foundation
Clitheroe Foundation
Jinnie & Ross Gavin
Ingrid Kaiser
Graham McConnochie
Neilson Foundation
Jenny Reynolds & Guy Reynolds AO
George & Diana Shirling
Southern Steel Group Pty Ltd

PLATINUM $20,000+

The Balnaves Foundation
Graham Bradley AM & Charlene Bradley
Clitheroe Foundation
Ingrid Kaiser
Graham McConnochie
Neilson Foundation
Alicia Powell
Jenny Reynolds & Guy Reynolds AO
Southern Steel Group Pty Ltd
Christine Thomson

GOLD $10,000+

Diane Balnaves
Darin Cooper Foundation
Jinnie & Ross Gavin
Steve & Julie Murphy
George & Diana Shirling
John & Diana Smythe Foundation
Jane Tham & Philip Maxwell

SILVER $5,000+

David Z Burger Foundation
Peter Eichhorn & Anne Willems
Ellimo 2 Family Trust
Garry, Debbie & Val
Alan Gunn
Matilda Hartwell
Emma Hodgman & John Coorey

James Family Charitable Foundation
Anne Elizabeth King
Merryn & Rod Pearse
Alan & Pauline Plumb
David Pumphrey OAM & Jill Pumphrey
Angus & Elspeth Richards
Lynn Trainor
Friends of Tracey Trinder
The Wenkart Foundation
Annie & Graham Williams
Liz Woolfson
Anonymous X 3

BRONZE $1,000+

Melanie & Michael America
Ellen Borda
Anne Bruning
Wayne Cahill
Lynette Casey & Patricia Zancancaro
Alison Carmine
Debby Cramer & Bill Caukill
Sue Donnelly
Jayati & Bishnu Dutta
Hon Ben Franklin MLC
Vivienne Golis
Tim & Jill Golledge
Diane Grady & Christopher Komor
Andrew & Wendy Hamlin
The Hilmer Family Endowment
Fiona Hopkins & Paul Bedbrook
Jacqueline Katz
John Lewis
Peter Lowry AM & Dr Carolyn Lowry OAM
Michael Markiewicz
Catriona Morgan-Hunn
Barbara Osborne
Georgie Parker
In Memory of John Power
Jim & Maggie Pritchitt

Ronald Sekel
Megan & Tim Sjoquist
Holly Stein
Bob Taffel
Geoffrey Tebbutt
Wendy Trevor Jones
Julia Wokes
Gavin M. Wong
In memory of John & Vanda Wright
Anonymous X 1

COMMISSIONERS' CIRCLE

Supporting new Australian work
Diane Balnaves
Graham Bradley AM & Charlene Bradley
Paul Clitheroe AM & Vicki Clitheroe
Jennifer Darin & Dennis Cooper
Ingrid Kaiser
Steve & Julie Murphy
Alicia Powell
Jenny Reynolds & Guy Reynolds AO
George & Diana Shirling
Jane Tham & Philip Maxwell
Christine Thomson

LEAVE A LEGACY

We would like to thank the following Estates for their generous donations
Estate of Freddie Bluhm
Estate of Helen Gordon
Estate of Leo Mamontoff
Estates of Zika & Dimitry Nesteroff
Estate of Margaret Stenhouse

ENCORE CIRCLE

Thank you to the following people for bequests in their wills:
Mark Midwinter
Joe Sbarro
Anonymous x 7

OUR PARTNERS

Thank you to our partners for playing a vital role in our success.

MAJOR PARTNER

THE
BALNAVES
FOUNDATION

ASSOCIATE PARTNER

NEILSON
FOUNDATION

STRATEGIC PARTNER

SOUTHERN
First for Steel

SUPPORTING PARTNERS

AKCS
www.akcs.com.au

AUDIO VISUAL EVENTS

BLOOMINGALES
LIFESTYLE STORE

Hungerford Hill

KAY & HUGHES

KENNARDS
HIRE

SPS. Sydney
Physio
Solutions

ENSEMBLE ED PARTNERS

Clitheroe
Foundation

FOOD
BANK
FIGHTING HUNGER
IN AUSTRALIA

The Smith
Family
everyone's family

ENSEMBLE THEATRE TEAM